AUTHENTICITY
IN MUSIC

RAYMOND LEPPA

AMADEUS PRESS

Reinhard G. Pauly, General Editor

Portland, Oregon

First published in 1988 by Faber Music Ltd
in association with Faber & Faber Ltd
3 Queen Square London WC1N 3AU
Design and typography by James Butler
Typeset by Andek Printing (London)
Music examples by Paul Broom
Cover design by M & S Tucker
Printed in Great Britain by
Halstan & Co Ltd
All rights reserved
© 1988 by Raymond Leppard

First published in North America in 1988 by
Amadeus Press
9999 SW Wilshire
Portland, Oregon 97225, USA

ISBN 0-931340-20-9

CONTENTS

CHAPTER ONE

THE NEW LISTENING

We live at a time when on any day, at any hour, by merely turning a knob we can expect to be able to hear music composed before 1800. Something by Monteverdi or Cavalli; something by Vivaldi, by Handel, by a Scarlatti (either of them) or a Bach (any of them), something by Haydn or Mozart, or almost anything by one of their lesser relations or contemporaries. Nothing is likely any longer to surprise us by its rarity or make us gasp, except for its intrinsic beauty – supposing we have the time to listen to it.

We may not recognize the music we hear but we're likely to be intrigued and curious to know its name. Many of us could have a fairly good shot at placing it in its period and country within the last 380 years. Right or wrong, this guessing game that most of us regularly play has become one of the most widespread of musical diversions; and, it must be emphasized here, a uniquely twentieth-century one. We have come, for the greater part unquestioningly, to regard as normal listening the huge historical span of music that is now so readily available. But it is not so generally realized how recent a phenomenon this is. A few facts, selected at random, may serve to illuminate this development, and point the direction for further discussion as to how it came about and how it has so profoundly affected and conditioned our attitudes to the art of music.

For those who are captivated by the music of early seventeenth-century Italy it is hard to believe that it has only been heard again with any frequency within the last 20 to 30 years.

Monteverdi's opera *L'incoronazione di Poppea* (1642) was given its first professional performance in England at Glyndebourne in 1962; *Il ritorno d'Ulisse* (1641) in 1971. In America, *Poppea* was first heard in 1963, performed by the Dallas Civic Opera; *Il ritorno* in 1974 by the Washington Opera Society.

Even in its skeletal, *Urtext* form the (almost) complete corpus of

Monteverdi's music has only been available in print since 1942, when the last volume of Malipiero's great editorial project, begun in 1926, was published.

A recording of some of Monteverdi's madrigals was made in 1937 under the direction of Nadia Boulanger, a result of her new-found enthusiasm for his music. Disregarded when it first came out, it has since become something of a classic, and was almost certainly the first recording of any of the composer's music.

Cavalli's opera *L'Ormindo* (1644) was performed for the first time in over 300 years at Glyndebourne in 1967, as was *La Calisto* (1651) in 1970. *L'Egisto* (1643) and *L'Orione* (1653) saw the light of day again at Santa Fe Opera in 1974 and 1983 respectively.

Virtually nothing by Vivaldi was heard in the nineteenth century or before the First World War. Only one or two violin concertos, made to sound as if composed by Max Bruch, were found to be useful for opening recital programmes, and achieved a certain currency among some of the more adventurous soloists.

Between the wars a few more concertos were exhumed, slowly releasing a crescendo of interest that reached its zenith after the Second World War when Renato Fasano and the Virtuosi di Roma (founded in 1952, the first of several such groups) based their successful careers on the seemingly endless supply of Vivaldi's music that became available in a collected edition begun in 1947. With over 600 instrumental works to be revived, it is scarcely surprising that first performances since the eighteenth century became more the rule than the exception, but this encouragement was hardly necessary in the tidal wave of enthusiasm for his music that has yet to abate.

The case of Handel is somewhat different, particularly in England where the northern choral societies flourished wonderfully during the nineteenth century, satisfying a deep need for spiritual comfort and uplift amid the grimy drabness of the industrial revolution. Apart from specially composed works by Mendelssohn, Dvořák and contemporary English composers, some of Handel's oratorios were regularly performed. However, as Winton Dean points out, 'we are apt to over-rate nineteenth century England's knowledge of Handel. Although performances of the oratorios were innumerable, with a few exceptions (mostly at the instance of amateur bodies like the Sacred Harmonic Society) they were confined to the same three or four works.'[1] Certainly no opera by Handel was heard at that time, except for a few arias usually adapted to sacred words.

Some did not like Handel at all. In 1907 Ernest Walker denounced 'the acres of complacent commonplaces, devoid alike of invention and workmanship'.[2] Mr Cuthbert Harris, writing in *Musical Opinion* in 1900, was not alone in thinking Handel's methods 'childlike and lacking variety of resource' and his limitations 'more marked than those of perhaps any other composer of equal standing. His music is almost entirely mechanical with its veneer of eighteenth century sentiment.' Even Sir Hubert Parry considered that 'Handel, accepting the conventions of Italian art without hesitation, ruined an enormous number of his works by the emptiest, baldest and most superficial formulae.'[3] It is inconceivable that similarly responsible musicians would either venture, or could possibly hold such opinions today. Understanding why this is so, and why such views were possible at the turn of the century, lies at the root of our considerations.

Handel's instrumental music and operas have a much more sharply defined starting point for revival. The sonatas, suites and concertos began to appear between the wars, when the harpsichord was revived for concert use.

After Handel's death, no opera of his was heard anywhere in Europe until 1920, when *Rodelinda* was produced at Göttingen. In 1953 the London Handel Opera Society was founded, and 18 of the operas they have produced to date have been first London productions since the eighteenth century. If any more striking example were needed, the first Handel opera ever professionally produced in America was *Giulio Cesare*, performed in 1965 at Kansas City and revived with great success by New York City Opera in 1966.

There is still much of Alessandro Scarlatti's music awaiting twentieth-century performance, but there are few music-lovers now (unlike the great majority of those in our grandparents' day) who can say they have never heard of him, or a note of his music. If any such there be, the admission would be ruefully made, with no implication that they had done very well up to now without the composer or his music – an opinion that would have caused no raised eyebrows at the beginning of the century.

Domenico Scarlatti published only one volume of harpsichord pieces in his lifetime. A number of the more difficult sonatas were known in the nineteenth century, serving as starters or encores at recitals by keyboard virtuosi like Tausig or Scharwenka, who adapted them to suit and show off their own particular technical

3

skills. By 1906 Alessandro Longo had edited and published six volumes containing 300 of Scarlatti's 550-odd sonatas and eventually, with the advent of harpsichordists like Wanda Landowska and Ralph Kirkpatrick, much of the complete opus entered the general listener's experience.

After J.S. Bach died in 1750 his music virtually ceased to exist for the rest of the eighteenth century. In Charles Burney's gigantic four-volume history of music completed in 1789, he is referred to in only four sentences: 'In organ-playing and composition, Handel and Sebastian Bach seem not only to have surpassed their contemporaries, but to have established a style for that instrument which is still respected and imitated by the greatest organists in Germany.'[4]

'Among organists of the present century, Handel and Sebastian Bach are the most renowned. Of Handel's performance there are still many living who can remember the grandeur, science and perfection; and Sebastian Bach is said, by Mr Marpurg, to be many great musicians in one: profound in science, fertile in fancy, and in taste easy and natural.'[5]

'The great Sebastian Bach, music-director at Leipzig, no less celebrated for his performance on the organ and compositions for that instrument, than for being the father of four sons, all great musicians in different branches of the art.'[6]

'If he had been possessed of the simplicity, clearness, and feeling of Handel, he would have been a greater man.'[7]

And that is the sum of attention Bach and all his music merited from the closest of scrutineers towards the end of the eighteenth century.

In fairness it must be said that through the enthusiasm and influence of S.S. Wesley, Burney came, by the end of his long life, to have a slightly deeper knowledge and respect for J.S. Bach. Wesley's enthusiasm, too, accounted for one of the first public manifestations of Bach's music in England, a single concert in 1809 at the New Rooms, Hanover Square. Illustrating the principle that one swallow does not make a summer, it was not well attended and Bach's name scarcely appears again in London until the 1830s. In September 1837, largely due to Mendelssohn's influence, the 'St Anne' Prelude and Fugue and a duet from the *St Matthew Passion* were performed at the Birmingham Festival. (In 1829 Mendelssohn had performed the passion in Leipzig for the first time since the composer's death.) A reviewer, with a not unknown lack of perception, found the duet 'a laboured production, unvocal and unfit for the words'.[8]

The enthusiasm of individuals persisted intermittently, resulting in the first English performance of the *St Matthew Passion* in April 1854, but public apathy and critical antagonism continued. In London, the Bach Choir was formed in 1875 expressly to perform the B Minor Mass, which it did for the first time in 1876. Jenny Lind – whose husband, Otto Goldschmidt, conducted – sang in the choir, and remarked afterwards, 'to think that an old woman like me, who has lived in music all my life, should have been told of this music by an amateur.'[9] North of the border, due perhaps to Scots caution, the Mass had to wait until 1908 for its first performance.

In Germany the Bach Gesellschaft, founded in 1850, began publishing Bach's complete works in 1851: for subscribers only and, for the most part, only in score without performing material. The edition was completed in 1896, providing a solid textual basis for the great revival of Bach's music that has occurred since the First World War. In 1888 the *Musical Times* had observed that 'it seems as though the time is coming when it will be still more widely appreciated' and, indeed, Bach now brings audiences into concert halls all over the world.

The music of Bach's sons has taken even longer to reach the public ear. Few people knew their names at the beginning of the century. But now they are more staple listening fare and their differing styles, their personalities and even their places in the family tree are more widely perceived.

Haydn fared almost as badly. In the 1906 *Grove*, C.F. Pohl could write 'there is still no complete edition of Haydn's symphonies. Many still remain in manuscript' – and therefore unheard. Now there are complete recordings and, thanks to the scholarship and indefatigable enthusiasm of Robbins Landon, a complete edition with accompanying orchestral material.

When I was at school during the last war I would go anywhere to hear one of the earlier symphonies. 'La Chasse', 'Mercury', 'Passione', 'Trauer'; these and their unnamed fellows were known to us as names or numbers only through biographies and dictionaries. Scores were generally unobtainable, there were almost no recordings, and the 'London' symphonies arranged for piano duet were our only means of partially discovering what is now so widely heard, the greatest single manifestation of eighteenth-century symphonic thought. And that was only 40 years ago.

5

Mozart's *Idomeneo* was given its first professional performance in England at Glyndebourne in 1951. It was heard at the Metropolitan Opera for the first time ever in 1982. *Così fan tutte* was first heard there (with very scant success) for a few performances in 1922 and *Il Seraglio* in 1946. *La Clemenza di Tito* was not heard in New York until 1984.

Such rehearsal of facts becomes tedious, and excessive repetition of the point they make blunts its impact. But we can now hear any of this music whenever we will. If concert-hall, opera-house and radio fail us there is always the gramophone, and, finding this very satisfying, we are not prone to question how it was, so short a time ago, when such variety was unknown. Nor do we often consider what our forbears would have made of the present situation. Yet the most significant aspect of any historical period lies in its unquestioned attitudes, and it is in these assumptions that we may see our own period most clearly revealed.

Few question the values that earlier music brings us. Its worth is recognized, but the questions raised about its performance rarely include why this is now so, and why the music is of such profound concern to us. To pause and consider how this passion for older music has come about may bring some focused understanding of its place in our aesthetic – and some resolution to the vexed question of authenticity which has become a blinkered, faddish pursuit among so many performers, listeners and critics, without the understanding of how and in what ways it may be valuable.

CHAPTER TWO

THE OLD LISTENING

We may at first feel some concern, some regret that our grandparents and great-grandparents were deprived of the enormous wealth of pre-1800 music so readily available now for daily listening. But we should be wasting our sympathy. That they would have been amazed by it is certain; that they would have been pleased by it is extremely unlikely. In all probability they would have regarded it as an unwelcome imposition of an eccentric, unsophisticated taste that had no business to occur and which held no real interest for them. The vast corpus of that music we have come to know and love they would have found fustian and quite dislikable, with little or no relevance to the present art of music as they knew and loved it.

Our forebears felt little need to look for values in earlier periods, all of which they believed to be inferior in most ways to their own. Such was the power of the idea of Progress. Life was generally understood to have improved to such an extent that almost any aspect of the past – social, scientific and artistic – was only even remotely interesting to the degree it could be said to have presaged the present. Like old clothes in a wardrobe, it was better discarded for fear of moths.

As far as actually listening to music was concerned, they heard much less than we do and probably listened harder and thought more about what they heard. Gramophones were experimental, concerts were rarer and much more of an event. They mainly heard music of their own time or such as immediately led up to it. Almost everyone subscribed to either the conservative Brahmsian school or the more advanced one of Wagner, and this was regarded as a laudatory example of a liberated society's refusal to accept superficial uniformity.

Each side traced and, with some pleasure, listened to composers who could be said to have made possible the work of those two main upholders of late nineteenth-century excellence. On one side were Schubert, Schumann and Mendelssohn; on the other were Weber and Liszt. Each protagonist had his acceptable contemporaries:

Dvořák, Reger and Bruch for the one, Bruckner, Humperdinck and Hugo Wolf for the other. Both sides could trace their lines back to Beethoven as the great original who made it all possible. He was therefore added to their lists of composers worth listening to, but only in works such as the Seventh Symphony or the 'Emperor' Concerto, that could safely be recognized as 'influential'. And they were generally played in an 'influential' manner. In this way was Beethoven regarded by the nineteenth century as an essentially Romantic composer.[1] His more Haydnesque music was ignored. The late quartets, together with the Missa Solemnis and the Ninth Symphony, were considered as somewhat hindered, visionary material for a Holy Grail yet to be fashioned at some future time. With Beethoven, the retrospective line of performable composers virtually came to an end.

A few works by Mozart, mostly in minor keys, were heard, though rarely. They were mainly of interest for the way they could be interpreted as precursors of the Romantic movement or identified as being by a composer, neglected in his short lifetime, who suffered and died in penury for his art. Haydn's long, cheerful and successful life did not fit him in any way for such interested concern and his music was largely neglected, except perhaps for *The Creation* which persisted a little, especially in the north of England. Almost nothing of Bach was generally played, except in the organ loft or on the G string. Apart from *Messiah* Handel was best known for a *Largo*, an 'Harmonious Blacksmith', and the legend that, as a child, he had had to practise his spinet secretly in an attic by candlelight because of a stern father's injunction against playing it at all.

The rest of music before 1800 was virtually unheard, unknown and unobtainable. There were very many and prolific nineteenth-century composers of every level and sort for salon, church, opera-house or concert-hall, so that our forbears were not short of music to listen to. It did not, in any case, take up anything like the time in daily life that it does now. Everyone was too busy improving themselves and their society to feel very strongly the need to stand, stare and listen to something that would alleviate present cares and doubts. Certainty of man's future and confidence in his ability to reach out and shape it was the prevalent mood of the civilized world in 1900.

The idea of Progress had taken about 300 years to develop into the immensely powerful, all-pervading force that dominated the opinions and outlook of our forbears in almost every aspect of living and thought. It was for them virtually beyond questioning. There is hardly space for, or purpose in, tracing at length the stages by which the idea grew into so comprehensive a philosophy. But classical authority had begun to be challenged at the end of the sixteenth century. Copernicus, Galileo and Kepler put an end to Ptolemy's belief that the earth was at the centre of things celestial; Newton discovered gravity; Drake and Champlain, following the lead of Columbus, Pizarro and Magellan, discovered the New World; Descartes discovered himself and came to rely on the discovery. Francis Bacon saw that the 'great renovation of knowledge' was not, as the Greeks had held, for the satisfaction of the mind, but enabled man to gain control over nature, the world and, therefore, his own destiny.

This was only the beginning of a chain of continually overthrown authority and an accretion of knowledge in all areas that led the late nineteenth century to believe it had progressed so far that heaven on earth was at least a ponderable possibility: to some, nearly a present reality; to others, ground for untrammelled optimism and a sense of superiority over all times past.

As Herbert Spencer wrote, 'It will be seen that as in each event today, so from the beginning, the decomposition of every expended force into several forces has been perpetually producing a higher complication; that the increase of heterogeneity so brought about is still going on and must continue to go on; and that thus progress is not an accident, not a thing within human control, but a beneficent necessity.'[2] 'The ultimate development of ideal man is logically certain – as certain as any conclusion in which we place the most implicit faith.'[3]

Backed by the evidence of the flood of scientific discovery, man clearly was close to complete control of his own future, even to those who regularly attended church or synagogue to thank a benevolent Deity for allowing them to come so far along the path of Progress towards a time when all things would indeed be bright and beautiful. They had, it was reasoned, come a great distance and laboured long and hard for their reward. Music was no less under the sway of this optimistic certainty than the sciences or philosophy, and the idea of Progress when applied to the art produced ways of thinking and systems for writing about it that have persisted, not always consciously, long after the original idea was abandoned.

That sort of certainty always seeks corroboration, and to sustain itself the idea of Progress inevitably needed the supporting evidence of a past from which it came, as well as a future towards which it was going. As far as future progress was concerned, the image of the Romantic composer was ideally suited to the idea. He was a man apart, remote, dreaming dreams, cherishing the public image of mystic incomprehensibility (although it must be said that all the best ones had a shrewd, clear eye to present success as well) and prone to making fairly obscure, seer-like statements about his work and music in general.

Best of all at this was Wagner, who wrote a celebrated book called *The Artwork of the Future* in 1850, part of a gigantic literary smoke-screen he created after having deserted in 1848 his fellow revolutionaries in Dresden where they had fought unsuccessfully for a united Germany. A year earlier Marx, under the influence of Comte, had produced his *Communist Manifesto*, and Wagner had become caught up in the egalitarian fervour. Once safely ensconced in Switzerland he began to write about it as far as it affected him, his art, and the part this should play in society.

Taking the ideas of Feuerbach (a favourite of Marx)[4] he projected the image of a classical Greece where the drama united poetry, mime and music. In the barbarous Middle Ages, to say nothing of decadent Roman times (the twists and turns the long line of history was forced to follow were many and varied) the unity of the classical drama was shattered and the elements dispersed. The subsequent progress of music's history has been to restore and surpass this classical unity. 'It must be born anew, not born again', 'Only the great Revolution of mankind can win this Art for us, an art that shall bring back a profound sense of beauty to all.'[5]

These writings by Wagner were at the heart of a strong force dominating European thought which drove men more and more towards self-reliance, towards learning their own importance, needs and desires so that out of their efforts could come ideal worlds of thought, deed and faith. Christianity and the older faiths became gradually nominal in this view and in man, common man – the *Volk* in Wagner's classification – was where the hope for the world's future lay.

Such woolly views, however passionately he would have defended them, were but supports for Wagner to come to his acts of creation, but they led him not only to folk-legends for inspiration in opera but also to his explanation of the future art-work's development. It would be the apotheosis of man's artistic endeavour and, hopefully, was not so far from being achieved. Certainly it would come within his own lifetime.

Wagner outlined an historical thesis of music, which he developed in *Opera and Drama* (1852), representing the muses sailing through the centuries of history on a sea that divided two continents, those of dancing and of poetry. Somehow the early Christians had lost themselves upon the sea of harmony, as exemplified by Palestrina who showed response neither to the word nor to the dance. In the seventeenth century the rise of secular music and the cultivation of the dance entailed further sailings from shore to shore until Beethoven, 'the chosen master who was, in his works, to write the world history of music'. Arriving on one shore, with the Sixth Symphony he stops to observe Nature; and then in the Seventh he composes the 'apotheosis of the dance'. Setting forth again he arrives at the opposite shore where 'resolutely he threw out his anchor, and this anchor was the *word*' – so accounting for the Ninth Symphony. 'Beyond this lay only the Complete Artwork (*Gesamtkunstwerk*) of the Future, the Universal Drama to which Beethoven has forged for us the artistic key.'

It is hard to believe that people would accept such child-like nonsense, but Wagner's writings were widely read and, fitting as they did into the accepted view of man's developing past, optimistic present and shining future, they were not without influence. Nor was his by any means the most fanciful conjecture of music's future. It took many forms, but everyone believed that in all likelihood it would reveal new heights, new splendours as yet unknown, the fruits of a long past and a glorious present, with Brahms and Wagner as bearers of the flame.

Wagner died in 1883, Brahms in 1897. There were no obvious successors to carry the torch forward into the twentieth century, but the philosophical climate and the momentum behind it meant that hopes ran high and there was no immediate doubt that the glorious progress of music would continue alongside that of science and society. Nor would there be until the guns of the First World War had begun to take their toll of optimism, as well as of men and women.

William Rockstro, concluding his very influential *General History of Music* of 1886, laments the death of Wagner. He had only twice mentioned Brahms, relegating him, together with Schumann, Bruch and Dvořák, as part of the 'last phase but one of [German music's] development'.[6] Music had at this point 'fairly reached the threshold of the latest phase of all . . . which passed its culminating point within the memory of men who have not yet grown old.'[7] Wagner is dead. But, 'granted that we are without a leader, . . . does it necessarily follow that no such leader is living among us, even now, unknown; learning his gamut perhaps in a garret in Soho as Beethoven learned his at Bonn? Can we be sure that he is not already at work in London or Paris or Dresden?' 'No one can foretell the nature of change that may and in all probability will, take place before the first morning of the twentieth century dawns upon the world. But the signs of the times all point in the direction of solid progress.'[8]

Even so dyspeptic an historian as Ernest Walker cannot escape the optimism. 'No doubt we have slept the sleep of the dull too often and too long; but now we are awake again. Nearly seven hundred years ago we gave to the world the first artistic music it had ever seen; who knows that we may not be its leaders once more?'[9] Sir Hubert Parry in 1896 gave another slant to the optimism: 'The resources are so immense, that none but composers gifted with special vital energy and power to grasp many factors at once, seem likely to use them to the full.'[10] 'It rests with a very wide public now to decide what the future of the art shall be. Though a man's life may not be prolonged, it may be widened and deepened by what he puts into it; and any possibility of getting into touch with those highest moments in art in which great ideals have been successfully embodied, is a chance of enriching human experience in the noblest manner: and through such sympathies and interests the humanising influence which mankind will hereafter have at its disposal may be infinitely enlarged.'[11]

No one writing about music now would openly venture such optimistic conjecture. But it might be profitable to consider whether we have entirely shed the trappings of the idea that music is progressing towards goals glimpsed by only a few, but more valuable on that account. As representatives of the few such visionaries one might cite those contemporary composers who appear to write more for a discerning future than for a responsive present. The idea that value somehow accrues to music that does not communicate in its own time can prove something of a refuge for lesser lights, as well as a danger not always sufficiently understood or guarded against by the more talented. The system of state-financed music that exists throughout Europe seems to encourage composers to continue this Romantic dream.

Of course, the most significant figures do take present communication seriously and search for ways of transmitting their creative images in recognizable form to establish contact with their own public. But there still exists the critical (and administrative) fallacy that obscurity

12

and technical innovation are themselves talismans of worth. (It is hard, for example, to imagine a conservative composer like J.S. Bach receiving, nowadays, a state subsidy, although with so large a family it is likely that he would have needed one.)

The 'glimpsed-at goal' has adversely affected the work of a number of composers, most sadly of all, perhaps, that of Arnold Schoenberg, a seminal influence in twentieth-century music. He considered that his compositions after the invention of his 12-tone system formed not the end of an old era but the beginning of a new one. In some ways he was right; but after 60 years, it is his earlier music that still communicates its fervid, hot-house, *fin de siècle* vitality with striking power, while his 12-tone music remains, for the most part, stubbornly in the head and on the page. The same composer was there all the time, but like one of the *penitentes* he seems to have whipped the emotion out of himself, leaving his influence as a teacher and, at the end, an embittered composer living impecuniously in the Los Angeles smog, while the great communicator, Igor Stravinsky, breathed the more expensive airs at the top of the hill.

This will not, I hope, be interpreted as a sanction, a plea for music that sets out only to divert and appeal with the minimum of effort expected on the part of the listener. High art will never be really easy of access, but it must have an element, a degree of initial communication involving the listener or else we shall not find our way to it. No longer does it count to say 'a time will come'. If we do not manage it in our time it seems no longer much comfort to say our children's children will understand. Every new work by Beethoven – even as he retreated further and further into his obscure, introverted, deaf world – was eagerly awaited by his contemporaries, whom he still managed to involve despite the handicaps. The C sharp minor quartet was difficult to approach in 1826, and still is; but his contemporaries knew it, as we know it now, to be a most remarkable manifestation of the human spirit.

CHAPTER THREE

THE FRUITFUL PAST

Confirmation of music's progress by evidence of its past was a much more certain activity than by conjecture about its future improvement. As a consequence, research into music's origins increasingly occupied our musical predecessors during the nineteenth century. The number of histories of music grew apace with the new enthusiasm, setting out results and putting in place the conclusions derived from their discoveries. And as the idea of Progress formed and came to dominate society, attitudes towards the story of music's past changed because of it.

The earlier histories, strongly influenced by the French encyclopaedists, had been written to demonstrate, by their compendious universality, man's powers of reason more than his continual improvement. Among the earliest in English were those of Dr Charles Burney and Sir John Hawkins, their first volumes both appearing in the same year, 1776. They set the style for narrative history (which really did not exist before) that persisted until quite recently when the need for things comprehensive declined. The *New* (and surely the last) *Oxford History of Music*, which began publication in 1954, came to be divided into separate volumes dealing with different periods, themselves divided into topics dealt with in segments researched and expounded by various authors, and reflecting no overall view except in so far as co-ordination by a general editor provides one. The need to show the grander scheme of things is past, and not only because the subject matter has become too large. There is no longer a compulsion to consider music history as a long line of connected categories, composers and techniques. Separate subjects examined in detail and collected together to represent certain periods are today sufficient to constitute history.

For Burney things were quite different. The present, especially as it manifested itself in Italian opera, represented the best in music, the epitome of good taste. The past was an interesting and illuminating study rather than proof or even explanation of eighteenth-century excellence. There was, of course, a consciousness of its contrast with the contemporary cult of sensibility, elegance and form which prompted occasional censure and distaste, but in no way did his extensive research suggest a systematic pattern of music's improvement. As we have already observed, Burney ignored J.S. Bach not from dislike, but simply because he didn't know his music. (It wouldn't have made any difference if he had). He did come across some of Monteverdi's music but, not understanding the composer's intentions in the new style nor even the reasons for the way it was written down, thought very little of it. Comparing him to Peri and Caccini, he wrote: 'I am unable to discover Monteverdi's superiority . . . his counterpoint in two parts is more frequently deficient than in the other two composers.'[1] Josquin, whose music was available in a more complete form, he praised highly for its contrapuntal skills. He made no attempt to fit any of them into a grander scheme. The scale and scope of his musical curiosity were enormous, but his studies were intended to enhance the knowledge of mankind, not to prove the validity of any single point of view.

After Burney and Hawkins the flow of histories increased to a flood by the later nineteenth century: Forkel (1788-1801), Kalkbrenner (1802), Busby (1819), Muller (1830), Schilling (1830), Stafford (1830), Kiesewetter (1834), Hogarth (1835), Fischer (1835), Higgins (1838), La Fage (1844), Blondeau (1847), Bird, the first in America (1850), Ambros (1862-82), Andries (1862), Hullah (1875), Trambusti (1867), Fétis (1869), Mendel (1870), Grove (1879), to mention only a few of the more important ones. Little by little, through this maze of print, music's past came to be viewed as a long, connected line steadily moving towards some ideal future. The historical evidence was woven, adapted, strengthened, even occasionally amended as the parallel awareness of man's continued progress in medicine, communication and the useful, as well as the purer sciences, seemed to fill the world with optimism. The pressure to make music fit into that general scheme was irresistible. Most historians of the late nineteenth century found themselves in willing accord, and able to justify their view one way or another.

Among the various solutions to the obvious problems of treating music's past in this way, and one of the most influential ones, was Sir Hubert Parry's *The Art of Music*, first published in 1893 and revised in 1896 as *The Evolution of the Art of Music*. It reached its tenth edition in 1931 with extra chapters by H.C. Colles, who then published his own version of the same philosophy, designed for schools, under the appropriate title *The Growth of Music* – still found in educational establishments today. Parry was strongly influenced by the writings of Herbert Spencer, whose optimistic views of man's future are quoted above in Chapter II. Darwin had proposed the idea of biological progress in his *Origin of Species* (1889), and the ever-increasing complexity of compositional techniques, size of orchestras, variety and range of instruments combined to persuade Sir Hubert that Spencer was right even as far as music was concerned. It had, he was sure, developed from simple, separate elements (primitive cries, scales, folk dances and what he calls 'incipient harmony') which had become more and more complex and integrated until the resources were now so considerable that only the greatest minds could fully use them. With Wagner and Brahms only lately deceased it was not unthinkable that a new genius would soon come along to bear the torch.

There were problems in the exposition of this view, for along the line of connected development there were those figures whose greatness could not be denied – although at the end of the nineteenth century these were fewer than today. For Parry and his contemporaries they were Palestrina, Bach, Handel, Haydn, Mozart and Beethoven. His solution to the problem was to accord each of them the accolade of qualified greatness, greatness with a 'but' generally not of their own making but imposed on them by the conditions of their era. Palestrina's 'but' lay in the fact that he lived at a time when he could only cultivate contrapuntal skills (which he did to a degree almost unique in the history of the art) and was deprived of the use of rhythm. In the Spencerian sense, music was still at a time when its elements were separated and the 'higher complications' had not yet enough affected him. For believers in Progress it reflected at once the weakness and the strength of Christianity in its tendency towards homogeneity of thought. The vitality of secular music was needed to add the element that would produce Bach and Handel. The 'but' of their greatness lies in the general tenets Parry uses for assessing the degrees of music's advancement. The development of principles of design in music must inevitably wait upon the development of technique. Very little can be done with limited means of performance.[2] Each composer, then as now, added his mite to the resources of a growing art when he managed to do something new.[3] Bach and Handel's erstwhile reputations as poor orchestrators spring from this widely-held view. Parry somewhat exonerates the former. 'The very loftiness of Bach's character and artistic aims prevented his condescending to do some of the work which had to be done before modern music could be completely matured.'[4] But Handel doesn't get off so lightly. He 'did as little as it is possible for a great master to do in adding to the resources of the instrumental side of music. He looked to the present and finished up much as he began.'[5] Then there were the 'buts' of Bach's excessive contrapuntal complexity where it is not essential, and Handel's crude recitative already referred to in Chapter I.

So remarkable were the achievements of Haydn and Mozart that 'if the world could be satisfied with the ideals of perfectly organised simplicity without any great force of expression, instrumental art might well have stopped at the point to which they brought it.'[6] But, of course, it couldn't. In opera 'Mozart's instinct for design was too cautious to allow him to venture upon untried methods which might fit more closely to the dialogue and to the progress of the action.'[7] As a result 'such sorrows as Elvira's are not in any sense capable of being adequately expressed. It is in such situations that the utter inadequacy of the old operatic scheme becomes too conspicuously glaring.'[8] It's hard now to believe he meant it.

With Beethoven, Parry came to a figure known by his readers to be great through widespread aural experience, and his 'but' in the name of Progress is more muted and more difficult to rationalize. Parry may even have been a little less convinced of it himself. The composer is called the first of the modern masters who became 'the interpreter of the innermost joys and sorrows of all human creatures.'[9] 'It is a palpable fact to everyone that Beethoven's works sound fuller and richer than those of any composers since Bach.'[10] The use of the orchestra is better; the use of the piano is better; the coda is better; the scherzo is better; the subtlety of design and expression is better, but . . . 'after him the course of things naturally changed.'[11] Sir Hubert goes on to explain, 'Beethoven stands just at the turning point of the ways of modern art, and combines the sum of past human effort in the direction of musical design with the first ripe utterance of the modern impulse – made possible by the great accumulation of artistic sources – in the direction of human expression.'[12]

Therein lies Parry's 'but' for Progress. Beethoven was at once great in his own right and great as a prophet of more wonderful things to come. His ability 'to modify the average scheme of the design of instrumental works in accordance with the ideas which he felt he could artistically express was one of the features in his works which

18

indicated the direction in which art was to travel after him.'[13] Doubtless referring to Wagner's use of the *Leitmotiv* and Liszt's thematic metamorphoses, Parry notes that Beethoven's 'power of presenting the same subject in different aspects has a very important bearing on the nature of recent progress of the art.'[14] So strong were Beethoven's personality and achievement that the rest of the generation rebelled. 'The instinct of man was impelled to resent the conventions of form which seemed to fetter his imagination and began his wanderings and experiments anew.'[15]

Parry saw the development of music after Beethoven as showing itself in the exploration of technical means (Paganini on the violin, Liszt on the piano), and moving 'towards variety and closeness of characterisation',[16] culminating in the two latest and greatest exponents of the art, the one for purely instrumental music, the other for opera. Brahms 'for greatness of expression and novelty of treatment stands out absolutely alone.'[17] Wagner is throughout as much dramatist and master of theatrical requirements as musician. 'Of the method itself it may be said that it is the logical outcome of the efforts of the long line of previous composers, and the most elaborately organised system for the purposes of dramatic musical expression that the world has ever yet seen.'[18]

'The long story of the development of music is a continuous and unbroken record of human effort to extend and enhance the possibilities of effects of sound upon human sensibilities, as representing in a formal or a direct manner the expression of man's inner being.'[19] At present (that is, at the end of the nineteenth century) 'mankind seems finally to have full measure of almost unlimited materials available to illustrate anything he will.'[20] High hopes indeed, and on this optimistic note Parry ends his study of music and its progress up to 1893.

Sir Hubert was among the most widely admired and respected musicians of his time. Professor of Music at Oxford and Director of the Royal College of Music, his beliefs had great influence on several generations of musicians and music-lovers. They were, moreover, quite in accord with those of his contemporaries in the other arts and sciences, however differently expressed. Parry might have been speaking for any leading figure in any other discipline, substituting the appropriate subjects, when he wrote: 'the whole history of the Arts is mainly a continuous effort of artistically-minded human creatures to make the means and the methods for the expression of the inner impulses richer and more perfect.'[21] There was, in his day, very

19

little reason for doubting it.

From our standpoint, 90 years later, there are flaws in a system that results in assessing composers by a scale of ten in the Progress chart. The steps by which music progressed, a real *gradus ad Parnassum*, produce a whole series of over-simplified musical sequiturs: *opera seria* and the intermezzi; French overtures and the suite; Italian overtures and the symphony; the *da capo* aria and theatrical perdition; Haydn into Beethoven; Weber into Wagner; Schumann into Brahms. Few of these connections feature large in present-day musical thinking or education, but they once did and it is hard for us to believe it, so enormous is the gulf between our forefathers' philosophy of life and ours. *But* . . . it was so.

CHAPTER FOUR

HIROSHIMA AND AFTER

While Progress was a logical, even demonstrable fact it was accepted by virtually everyone without question or dissent. Various factors have contributed to its decline, but none so powerful or convincing as the two major European wars. It really was not easy to argue that the years between 1914 and 1918 were an improvement on those that went before; and if there were hope that they might eventually be considered and then dismissed as a temporary aberration as man continued his upward path into the twentieth century, the five years after 1939 effectively disposed of any such idea. Those, without doubt, were distinctly worse, especially 1945 with its atomic bomb which on 6 August shattered more than man's hopes of continued improvement.

Progress in science had, for the very first time, produced something that could destroy man and the entire world he lived in. Given his still imperfect moral condition, the likelihood that he would bungle matters, go ahead and do it became a vivid, universal fear, especially for younger people who had no pre-war funds of optimism to bolster disbelief that such a thing could ever come about. They knew that it could. They knew also that this, for sure, was not better in any way. A comfortable copy of the Celestial City on earth was one thing: to rekindle optimism and assuage fears after the blaze and brilliance of Hiroshima was quite another.

Among the older generations may still be heard an occasional faint bleat in support of Progress, but that's all it is. The real beliefs of our time have moved elsewhere. With them, attitudes to life and the living of it have also changed, and much more significantly than the influence of the Beatles or Michael Jackson might suggest, although they were and are manifestations of it. The ideas generated by the concept of Progress have no part in the present generation's attitudes, except they be unwittingly inherited from the past. The future is no longer something of promise, to leave one's mark on, to save for, worth striving for or even planning for, at least not beyond the children. Thereafter it has to be *their* problem.

The present is what mainly matters, for if and while we have it there is reason to be thankful. If right triumphs there is even reason to be hopeful for the next generation. The striving must be to keep it stable, live it as fully as we can and, in the process, search all the time for reassurances that it will go on. There is a new sort of faith possible in all this which much of the present generation is discovering: without it comes despair, recourse to violence, drugs, crime, sexual excess, protest or almost any escape from the unpalatable lack of foundation for living.

Fear of what he has done has truly changed man's mind; his predicament is not unlike Adam's in the Garden of Eden.

A faith destroyed needs another to replace it, for man is an incurable optimist. Sadly, the established churches have failed to realize this. Where they could have renewed waning interest they squabbled about language and format; where they could have involved through use of the arts they bored by experimenting with worthless trivialities; where they could have won minds by sympathy with contemporary problems like contraception, abortion and homosexuality, they retreated into synods and conventions discussing arid changes in doctrine and thus alienated intelligent interest. Worst of all, where they could have sustained by conviction they have seemed as daunted and amazed as any of us.

No one faith came to replace the older creeds. The single, binding factor was the fear and sense of peril. The search for reassurance took myriad different courses. Cults flourished as never before, all purporting to provide a solution, sustaining faith. Some, perhaps, achieve something along those lines; some use the needs of the young for their own profit. The more emotional, evangelical religions have fared better than the authoritarian ones. Some people, the more politically minded, make do with anti-nuclear marches and campaigns against various social injustices, real and imaginary. *In extremis* some take to terrorism.

More widespread than any of them, and more important because it can be incorporated in all of them, is the rediscovery of past values. This is no longer made with the intention of proving the present's superiority or the future's promise, but to seek confirmation that what has endured for years, maybe for centuries, and can still be counted valuable, would seem to suggest a sort of permanence when all else around shows very little indication of it. Old houses are visited

22

by thousands of people; old things are collected: furniture, silver, paintings, drawings, clocks, cars, cigarette cards, almost anything that bespeaks an older, enduring value.

Among the main enthusiasms has been, and still is, the rediscovery of old music, of music from the centuries before 1800. The realization that it is still able to communicate its vitality in present performance apparently undiminished by the intervening years has put music among the most vivid and potent instruments of hope that all is not and will not be lost, that some values are constant and likely to remain so.

Almost as if by divine intervention, the means to make this possible seemed to appear at the right time. To our forbears the radio was a minor amateur enthusiasm. Now everyone has one. Some countries have a 'third' programme, some a number of classical musical stations. The gramophone, invented at the turn of the century has evolved through 78, 45 and 33 revolutions to the latest compact disc, and everyone has one or other version of it. The sale of records is big business and the collecting of them, to say nothing of cassettes and video-tapes, a widespread passion. Many people collect more than they are likely to re-hear in a lifetime, but the very passion for them may have something in common with the taking of correspondence courses. They cannot themselves guarantee an education or a future but they both represent the wish to have one.

Orchestras, opera-houses and concert-halls flourish, and television, in its own way, has done its part, although it is mainly concerned with expectations of only a very short duration. At the same time as the proliferation of mechanical aids for the dissemination of music, and not unaffected by them, music has become, especially in Europe, a favoured instrument of education of great importance and on an unprecedented scale. The number and excellence of youth orchestras are evidence of much more widespread musical activities, an outward manifestation of the confidence educators now place in the power of music to inculcate moral as well as musical standards. Before 1914 music was not considered in that light. It was a suitable accomplishment for young ladies, perhaps, but hardly a part of serious education or of inherent value.

Ironically, the passion for music's rediscovery had already begun under the aegis of this philosophy. As the output of music histories increased during the nineteenth century, so did the need for accurate research, especially in Germany, a country noted for its enthusiasm for thoroughness. By the end of the century there had developed a breed of scholars who devoted their energies to unearthing the facts and musical texts of certain periods and topics. It was by no means a wide or popular movement, but by their researches men like Schilling, von Winterfeld and Goldschmidt painstakingly laid the foundations for future enthusiasms. They themselves had little interest in making their chosen fields more widely known through performance, and were largely innocent of the later effects their studies were to have.

That sort of impetus came from another type of scholar more commonly found in England: quasi-amateur, well-read, well-educated, often involved in other professions but with leisure and means to indulge their enthusiasms. J.A. Fuller Maitland and William Barclay-Squire rediscovered the *Fitzwilliam Virginal Book* and had it printed in 1899. The Rev. E.H. Fellowes enthusiastically brought the English Madrigal School back to life, to say nothing of Tudor church music. W.H. Cummings founded the Purcell Society with the aim of publishing and performing that composer's music, little of which had been seen or heard since the seventeenth century. Professor E.J. Dent wrote the first biography of Alessandro Scarlatti; F.T. Arnold made a large compilation of sources of instruction on the playing of figured-bass; H.E. Wooldridge wrote about earlier polyphonic music, Dom Anselm Hughes about plainsong. Scholars all, with an almost evangelical passion for sharing their enthusiasms by putting the music they admired back into sound as much as on to paper in histories or academic journals.

In this they were aided by the small, growing band of performers of the earlier music. Arnold Dolmetsch and his family come to mind, but there were many others: Carl Engel, Wanda Landowska, Violet Gordon-Woodhouse, Henry Watson and F.W. Galpin, to say nothing of more recent figures. Apart from their direct influence through teaching, they provided an aural climate and an example for the next generations. Publishers and their presses were not slow or unenthusiastic about joining in; men like Chrysander, Brahms, Saint-Saëns, Arkwright, William Chappell, Edward Rimbault and more anonymous groups like the German Bach and Handel societies, the Musical Antiquarian Society and the Plainsong and Mediaeval Music Society prepared edition after edition. By the years following the Second World War there was scarcely a note of any value left unpublished, and today there is scarcely a minor figure of any period who is not threatened with a complete edition.

The hunger for the discovering of earlier and still earlier music seems to be insatiable; but there is a limit, and we are reaching it. Before the ninth century, oral tradition was the most accurate, almost the only means of keeping music alive in performance. Up to the eleventh century there were only the vaguest symbols for pitch, and little that can be transcribed into usable modern notation was written down before the end of the thirteenth century. That, therefore, is as far back as the search for confirmation of artistic values in music can take us in any tangible way. But the need seems to be so strong that, although most of the ground between 1300 and 1800 has been covered (and in a remarkably short time), the search has turned in on itself and, like a toenail reaching the end of a shoe, is in danger of becoming ingrown.

CHAPTER FIVE

THE END OF THE LINE

Before notation there is virtually nothing to research or revive in music. Painting, sculpture, artefacts, architecture and literature can be examined in much earlier periods, and enthusiasts in these fields have by no means come to the end of the line. But music has, and with the basic need for confirmation in no way abated, the searching process has become extremely involuted with a veritable traffic-jam of eager, industrious scholars travelling back and forth along well-worn paths. The result is a number of very nasty accidents, as well as a good deal of spite and bad temper.

The block in music, as far as the general listener's ability to recognize value is concerned, occurs somewhat later than the beginning of notation. It may yet change, but mediaeval music, except where skilfully adapted for present-day audiences by a Noah Greenberg or a David Munrow, has not been widely appreciated. It serves for some, but has not so far elicited anything like so wide or vivid a response as that of music from the sixteenth and later centuries. All the same, scholars keep hunting high and low in the libraries of Europe and America, and the smallest newly-discovered canzona acquires for them an importance and value usually quite unrelated to its content. Many an academic or critical reputation has been made and lost by such discoveries, so intense is the search even in the most minor fields of musicology.

The same sort of intensity can be seen in all the arts. Not just the discovery of a piffling little fugue possibly by Bach, but a dull little poem possibly by Shakespeare has the media of the world in a frenzy of activity. The attribution (and the faking, formerly quite openly accepted as copying) of old masters has become notoriously big business. There are, for example, many more Canalettos adorning the walls of Europe and America than even that industrious painter could possibly have managed in one lifetime. The plethora of these paintings produced to satisfy a ravenous market for old masters reminds one of those pieces of wood sold as reliquaries in the mediaeval church. Put together, they would have built not just one cross, but several houses. Both, in their separate ways, became symbols of a future life.

The insurmountable impasse of notation, or rather the lack of it, before 1300 has caused responsible scholarship to abandon hope of making significant new discoveries. Instead, while lesser lights turn to the *minutiae* of musicology, the main thrust of research has been towards revealing the ways and means of past performance. In this manner would scholarship enable musicians to copy closely and reproduce exactly the way music was first heard in the hope that it will become still more real, still more valuable. It is, on the face of it, a most attractive idea.

There have been two clearly discernible results. On the one hand, research has contributed wonderfully to illuminating and giving greater insight and freedom to the bringing of older music back to present-day, sentient life. On the other, it has sometimes resulted in restriction and a sort of mean-spirited isolationism, promoting the formation of musical cults. Their exclusivity has in some cases seemed wilfully to impede the twentieth-century listener's access to the music, and even the performer's right to perform it, just as religious cults exclude those outside their beliefs from their sort of salvation.

Well before either of these trends could be distinguished, the process of exploring ways and means had begun under the aegis of historical accuracy, of proving origins and establishing a compendium of reliable evidence on which could be based the theory of music's continued development. This evidence proved easily adaptable to the changed needs of more recent years.

About the turn of the century, instruments moldering in houses and museums, known to have been part of earlier music's performance, began to be resuscitated; at first out of curiosity, then out of enthusiasm for the light they threw on the content of the music as well as the way it had been performed.

The clarity and pulse of a Scarlatti sonata played on the harpsichord eventually showed music-lovers that the music contained things different from those suggested by nineteenth-century virtuosi, beginning their recitals with a well-pedalled group of sonatas – played at speeds and in ways dictated more by technical accomplishment than by concern for the music's meaning, riveting as this approach may have been at a different level of comprehension. This is in no way intended to suggest that Scarlatti sonatas should not be played on the piano; only that the music, once heard on the earlier instrument for which it was composed, reveals aspects of itself that must affect its performance, no matter what instrument is eventually used.

The rediscovery of the harpsichord was initially associated with the arts-and-crafts movement in Europe, characterized also by a certain harmless, bizarre eccentricity associated with herbal remedies, country dancing, weaving, pottery and eclectic societies whose members were initially somewhat mocked by their more conventional contemporaries. Nevertheless the 'knit-your-own-violin' school achieved remarkable things and survived to take its place among the first of those who showed older values still valuable. Barely a National Trust house is now without a shop showing considerable evidence of their continued vitality and industry. Their particular enthusiasm bred, too, a gentle generosity of spirit that was apparent in their love for early music, on whose performance they had an almost wholly beneficial effect.

In England the Dolmetsch family, if not alone, were certainly the most celebrated of those early protagonists. Stories about them are legion, with a benevolently tyrannical father making all his large family play a great variety of instruments – harpsichords, virginals, spinets, clavichords, viols, recorders, lutes and sackbuts – some, it must be said, more successfully than others. The family began giving concerts of consort music in 1890 and in 1925 finally established themselves at Haslemere, giving an important annual series of concerts devoted to early music.

The inevitably rickety condition of instruments several hundred years old led to their being copied, and Arnold Dolmetsch made harpsichords, lutes and viols from the 1890s until his death in 1940; a similar movement in France had resulted in the first new harpsichord from Erard in 1882. Enthusiasm for the instrument and its fellows gained momentum and, apart from the restoration of such old instruments as were left in resuscitable state, more and more makers began to copy them, reviving old skills, sometimes combining them with modern scientific methods and discoveries. Reasonably enough there were jealousies, and the makers were not always charitable about each other. Dolmetsch was known for his sharp tongue and, a little later on, I never heard Hugh Gough say anything agreeable about his namesake, Tom Goff. Nor were Mr Hodgson or Mr Goble above an observation or two concerning their contemporaries. However, as a player in the 1950s one may have favoured one or the

29

other, yet there was never any real difficulty about playing any or all of their instruments, either technically or personally – beyond a sorrowful glance or a shake of the head. They were not exclusive.

Led by the work of two Americans, Frank Hubbard and William Dowd, a new sort of harpsichord began to be produced after the Second World War, and the change is significant.

In the name of authenticity they copied selected earlier instruments, and in building them reproduced exactly their narrow keyboards. Each key is only a matter of millimetres less than the standard keys common to all pianos and a large number of other earlier harpsichords. The narrowness makes no difference to the sound and is scarcely perceptible to the hands over small melodic intervals. Over several octaves, however, the smaller scale becomes an impossible obstacle to accuracy and virtually excludes the player accustomed to the larger keyboard from being able to use them.

Harpsichords, especially two-manual ones, have several ranks of strings which by the later eighteenth century were regularly brought in and out of action by the use of pedals, a great boon to the player whose hands tend to be fully occupied in, say, a busy piece by Rameau. Previously he would have had to bring on or release the various ranks of strings. thus changing the dynamics and colour, by using hand-stops which move levers to that effect. There can be little doubt that the invention of pedals to fulfil this function was an improvement of the player's lot and did not affect the sound of the instruments in any way. But Mr Hubbard and Mr Dowd regarded pedals as impure, for no very convincing reason beyond 'authenticity', and allowed only hand-stops on their instruments; a restriction for players tantamount to an infringement of the First Amendment.

In some quarters the practice of making useless 'authenticity' an excuse for further exclusivity continued and diversified, with lower-pitch instruments made of 'original' materials which virtually precluded them from playing with most other instruments. Mr Dowd and Mr Hubbard, having started their activities in tandem, had a falling-out and their disciples were divided. They in their turn began to produce instruments whose sources tended to become still more narrowly focused. Be they modelled on harpsichords by Ruckers, Taskin, Schudi, Haas or Kirkman, their creators, rather like high priests of a religious cult, seemed to be laying claim to have discovered the real way, the golden road, *le droict chemin* as Loys Bourgeois called an equally pious musical system in 1556, towards enlightenment and resolution of all stylistic problems. The makers had and have very little good to say of one another, which might perhaps cast doubts as to the universality of their solution, but they all have their followers.

Much the same has happened still more recently with almost every instrument that can be said to have been different at some earlier period of its history. Flutes, oboes, clarinets, bassoons, violins, violas, cellos, basses, trumpets, horns, trombones and timpani, all are now being produced in earlier forms, all in the name of authenticity, all showing fascinating technical features which will help renew attitudes to performance of the music for which they were originally used. The techniques for playing them are often radically different from those of their later counterparts, and generally they are played at a lower pitch – all of which tends to render the player less fit to play both sorts of instrument. This exclusivity also ensures less professional competition, and too often the less good players hide their technical and musical deficiencies under the mantle of 'authenticity' and sit behind their 'original' instruments bristling with insecure dislike of their colleagues in the professional mainstream.

What all these instruments can show when, as now is often the case, they are well played, are aspects of phrasing, articulation, rhythm, accentuation, rubato, speeds and dynamics that are wonderfully illuminating. They raise questions and generate ideas about the music they play that may never have occurred to the player accustomed to the instruments in their twentieth-century state, especially if these ideas, though stemming from the technical aspects of the instruments, are applied to the content of the music. It must be true that just to play a Handel oboe concerto on a Baroque oboe is no guarantee that deeper penetration of the music's significance will result. That can only come about through the mind, and through intuitive understanding; but these can be stimulated, and the understanding enhanced, by these technical differences between 'authentic' and twentieth-century instruments.

Another important result of the notational impasse to historical research has been the increased exploration of ways as opposed to means of performance. Books about the ways to perform early music began to be published early in the twentieth century. In 1916 Arnold Dolmetsch published his *Interpretation of the Music of the XVII and XVIII Centuries*, one of the first of many such exercises in stylistic explanation. More useful still has been the publication of original manuals about performance from all periods. In the 1890s Edward Dannreuther had produced what was essentially a two-volume précis of several such texts.[1] Now virtually all the important texts are available, enabling the student performer to come to his own conclusions as to the way his music should go.

Like a mirage in the desert, these glimpses of the ways certain music was originally performed may deceive one into thinking one has discovered the authentic oasis. But music is very difficult to write about, and the facts of performance almost impossible accurately to describe. Musicians, too, are not and never have been the most literate of beings. Their skills lie more with notes than words. Even so intelligent a man as C.P.E. Bach, in his *Essay on the True Method of Playing the Clavier* (1753), seems to have been incapable of explaining anything in a foolproof manner, and though what he writes is extremely valuable he is the first to admit that 'for every case covered even by the best rule there will be an exception.' François Couperin in *The Art of Playing the Harpsichord* (1716) describes with characteristic French *insouciance* ways of interpreting his own very individual system of ornamentation signs, and has left players tremulous in their uncertainty, or exaggeratedly assertive, ever since. As for fingering his pieces in the way he would seem to propose, this can only confirm the French propensity for being amused at the discomfort of foreigners.

All the same, these and dozens of other texts now readily available allow one to enter the period of the music they describe. Intelligently read with a certain objectivity, intuition, humour and a considerable ability for compromise, they can light as vividly as anything else the way towards informed performance of the music with which they are associated.

A third result of the impasse, and now a *sine qua non* for the renewal of vitality in our twentieth-century view of earlier music, is the publication of what Germans call the *Urtext*, the closest possible reproduction of the composer's manuscript. To have, as a starting-point for performance, the text of a piece of music as it first appeared on paper must be, without exception, the most important element in the complicated procedure that then follows before the music sounds. But this is not so simple as it would appear. Before the music is transformed from manuscript to print, editors, publishers and printers all have to make decisions that can vitally affect the result.

You have only to compare a Mozart manuscript with the latest editions to see questionable interpretations of unclear phrasemarks; decisions about where the *p* of a *sfp* mark should come (see the opening of the 'Prague' Symphony); how various editors have interpreted the differences in Mozart's *staccato* marks, a hideously difficult problem as the composer clearly indicates at least two sorts, but not altogether consistently and with confusing implications of how they should be interpreted.

The printed scores of the Schubert symphonies have been available since the late nineteenth century, and in performance many an opening or closing chord has begun loudly and diminished to *piano* because of a long, pointed sign ═══════ . The sign appears in the composer's manuscript, and to interpret it as a *diminuendo* is not at all unreasonable – until you discover in the body of the manuscript many cases of what are irrefutably accents, not *diminuendos*, written in exactly the same way. Berlioz also wrote long accents, with similar falsely contrived interpretative effects resulting from our tendency to believe what we see in print. The pitfalls are endless, and only a little less dangerous if you work solely from facsimiles of the composer's manuscript. You simply take the burden of deciding these matters on your own shoulder.

All this is to say that *Urtext* editions – like W.S. Gilbert's 'skimmed milk' – frequently masquerade as 'cream', and all too often reflect the foibles of an academic or a printer with little or no real intuitive understanding of the manuscript, the composer or the process and circumstances of performance it represents. These are most reliably gathered by people experienced in performance, capable of intelligent examination of the composer's score backed up by the widest possible knowledge of the rest of his music.

A fourth element contributory to the rejuvenation of the image of earlier music is the historical study of conditions for performance. To read in the *Mercure galant* of March 1683 that 'le Manche des Théorbes de l'orchestre cache toujours quelque chose de la vue' not only tells us something about the height of the orchestra pit, but also of the considerable numbers of theorbos still used for the continuo group in Venetian opera at that time. To look at the famous painting of an operatic performance at Esterházy shows the exact numbers of players Haydn was accustomed to work with there at that time. An engraving (1749) of the Palazzo Reale in Naples by Giuseppi Vasi shows an orchestra three times as large.

The material is endless and fascinating, serving to give an idea of numbers and scope which cannot help but influence the way we perform the music now. But to put performance therefore into rigid, factual straitjackets is fatal. Handel had many more players and singers for his performances of *Acis and Galatea* in London than in the version that was first heard at Cannons. Who, at this point in time, may say which is the better and, for want of first-hand evidence, which Handel preferred? Both may be convincingly argued, and both may serve to reveal the music's content.

Such variables are so common in the history of performance, composers themselves often being among the most adaptable of people, that it is fruitless to make rules and set absolute conditions for performance. There can be no reason why, for example, a Haydn opera composed for Esterházy should not be performed in a much larger modern theatre. But to insist in such surroundings on the tiny band that Haydn used may so diminish its effect as to cause the venture to fail. Sensitive judgement, rather than dogmatic statement, is called for.

More important still as part of this fourth element is the study of the culture that surrounds a period of music. The fact that Monteverdi must have known Rubens and his work over a period of seven or eight years (they were both at the small, Mantuan court of the Gonzagas between 1600 and 1608) cannot help but colour our attitude to his music. The plunging horses of *The Fall of Phaeton* (1605); the body of the drowning Leander, the falling Hero and the cupids, nymphs and naiads who try to help, a moment of pure theatre, in *Hero and Leander* (1606); the violence of *St George Fighting the Dragon* (1606); this extreme, superbly controlled sensuality must have struck sympathetic vibrations in the composer's mind as he explored the potential of *le nuove musiche*, and it surely must inform our performances of it now.

Purcell knew Dryden well and was painted by Kneller. Handel was a friend of John Gay and Alexander Pope, ate well and had a great collection of paintings, including two Rembrandts. Bach barely knew anybody except the severe Lutheran Church Councils where he worked, whom we, too, would do well to know.

It must surely be true that the closer we come to the literature, painting, theatre and society around the music, the more likely we are to be able to recreate the ethos in which it was written; more likely than through blind pursuit of fact, in the hope of pinning down the authenticity of a style like a butterfly to a board.

34

CHAPTER SIX

IN PRACTICE

As we have seen, there are four ways that musical scholarship has responded to the impasse in historical discovery: the revival of old instruments, research into the way composers evidently expected their music to be played, the publication of original texts, and the exploration of the society and culture that surrounded them. All of these pose a multitude of questions, both general in the consideration of music's place in our time, and highly specific when it comes to the performance of a single work, especially one of great significance.

Taking this as a cue, I propose to examine the processes by which three important, but very different, problematic pieces of music may be approached and realized in sound. No single way will be proposed, nor any claimed as best or most desirable. There are always too many variables for that, usually starting with the evidence of the earliest performances in the composer's lifetime. The aim must be to show the music's vitality and meaning to a late-twentieth-century audience – there seems no point in preparing it for any other purpose – so that they may find an equivalent sense of value in it, made the more valuable by having persisted for several hundred years.

My approach may illuminate for some, give courage to others, and offend a few. It will raise the eyebrows of those committed to purity and raise the level of venom in those predisposed to strike; but it is based on the actual experience of bringing these works to effective performance, and I stand by the methods and thinking that went into their preparation even if, because time has passed, I might change some details.

Gluck: *Orfeo*
For those seeking to produce an 'authentic' performance of Gluck's

Orfeo there is one obvious course to take. A gift to the unsuspecting and pure at heart, there is an original first version of the opera. A great deal has been written and said in approval of it, mostly by those who have not left their desks or entered the theatre before writing or saying it. They are persuaded of its superiority by the underlying conviction that to be first is to be best, whereas, even if we do not believe the Bible, we know this is not necessarily so. The only certain thing about being first is that that is what you are. This is as true of motor races as it is of Adam and of the first version of *Orfeo*. There is nothing intrinsically or more widely of value to be drawn from the fact.

The truth is that Gluck, already a composer of many successful but rather ordinary Italian operas, was persuaded in Vienna to undertake a somewhat revolutionary concept of the legend of Orpheus by a rather pushy, adventurer librettist, Raniero de' Calzabigi. That was in 1762. Gluck was no fool – he was ambitious, a *bon viveur* (he eventually died of apoplexy from overeating) and always looking for opportunities. He rose to the challenge and produced a remarkable score aimed at startling the Viennese into new appreciation of its author's talents.

Not remarkable enough, however, for the opera had scant success and scarcely produced more than a ripple on the wider European scene. It was put aside until 12 years later when, in 1774, the opportunity came to produce it in Paris. The venture was masterminded by Du Roullet, a clever and ambitious politician, attaché at the French Embassy in Vienna, friend of both Gluck and Calzabigi and the best P.R. man of his time. The idea was to translate, rework and adapt the first version of *Orfeo* for a French audience, and to sell the idea in advance. The link with Marie Antoinette (to whom, as a princess in Vienna, Gluck had taught singing, and who had gone to France in 1770) was an added encouragement.

The project's success enhanced Gluck's reputation as a composer of revolutionary operas that delighted the French for as long as there was scandal in them, and delighted Gluck for as long as there was money in them. A great deal of music was added to the original version, and of a marvellously theatrical quality; for Gluck had, it transpired, great gifts in that direction, even if he did have no more counterpoint than Handel's cook. The central character of *Orfeo*, first written in Vienna for the famous castrato Gaetano Guadagni, was altered, enlarged and transposed in Paris for the *haut-contre* (an extremely high tenor) of Joseph le Gros. This voice was popular with the French, who did not like the castrati for, presumably, Gallic reasons. Like the castrato, the *haut-contre* sound is almost unknown today.

Most of Gluck's adaptation and expansion for Paris of his earlier score can be stated categorically to be an improvement; and almost all of the items he added – the first aria for Amor, the great recitative and aria for Orfeo that ends Act I, the Dance of the Furies, the Dance of the Blessed Spirits, Euridice's ravishing 6/8 aria with chorus, the last trio and the splendid concluding chaconne – have rightly become celebrated and rated as among the best things in the opera. It seems to me, therefore, to come into the category of cutting noses to spite faces to do without them in the name of authenticity, academically interesting as it may be to see what Gluck and Calzabigi's first thoughts about the opera were. Only an opera buff blinded by an arrogant desire for exclusivity could possibly claim that it was better, or even a decently viable alternative to the later version. It must be remembered, causing our purist to wince perhaps, that at Parma in 1769 Gluck himself arranged the first version of the work for a soprano castrato, Giuseppe Millico, and, like all composers of almost any period before 1800, was quite used to making things work in differing situations.

Assuming the intention to produce the larger, later version, there are problems ahead that will cause the academic mind sleepless nights. Berlioz was the first to propound them and to provide a viable solution. The first problem for Berlioz was the *haut-contre*; the second his passion for the singer Pauline Viardot. The latter no longer matters very much but the present lack of *haut-contres* does. A high tenor under extreme pressure to sustain his line and retain intonation at so elevated a tessitura is a less likely personification of Orpheus, that strange, remote, spiritual singer of songs, than a castrato or a mezzo-soprano in travesty – an operatic convention that has played a large and successful part in the form since it started. Gluck himself found even le Gros' voice difficult to accept, and was said to have complained that sometimes it sounded like sawing through bones. Anguish, he is said to have observed, should be felt inwardly as if it came from the heart.

Berlioz' happy combination of passions resulted in a version based faithfully on the French version, with some transpositions – Orfeo's first strophic aria and subsequent recitative, his last aria in Act I (which Berlioz also rescored unnecessarily, including some monstrous cadenzas for his adored diva), the furies' scene, 'Che farò' (back to the key Gluck first used in Vienna) – and a very few adaptations in the recitatives, something any good professional could have accomplished without difficulty. Certainly nothing to bring blushes to the virginal cheeks of a purist, complicated as the small alterations involved in the transpositions are.

There is nowadays no reason not to reinstate the vivid colours of the two cor anglais, two clarinets (chalumeaux), two cornetti and harpsichord that were used so effectively in the original Viennese scoring, but which were not available to Gluck in the Paris of 1774 or to Berlioz in the Paris of 1866.

Berlioz performed the opera in French, as had Gluck in 1774. If you think the work sounds better in Italian then you may return to the Calzabigi text for the music of the original version and for the rest must choose between the various Italian translations that have been made since the 1774 version; for this was sung all over Europe, and frequently in Italian.

Today we have all this information and must come to our own solutions, our own compromises. To enshrine the solutions of Berlioz without question is simply to cement in ideas and attitudes of another period foreign to both Gluck's and our own. Very little 'tampering' is necessary; it is much more a matter of choosing with the 1774 Parisian score always in mind. Sir Charles Mackerras is mistaken in saying that this, Gluck's second version, is 'theatrically not viable'.[1] On the contrary, in it lies the authentic and most complete vision that Gluck presented to us, impossible as it is to put directly into practice. He is also in error in saying that the bravura aria of Orfeo that ends Act I, 'Addio, miei sospiri', is 'certainly out of keeping with the lofty character of the rest of the opera'.[2] It is out of keeping with Berlioz' high-Romantic view of the work, but not at all if we consider it in terms of the eighteenth century. It then wonderfully symbolizes Orpheus' new-found determination to conquer Hell in the search for his beloved Euridice, and Gluck, supremely able dramatist that he was, used it to give the end of Act I a powerfully energetic lift before the hero reappears at the beginning of Act II, now facing the dark portals of the underworld.

Lovingly, unafraid of compromise, never losing touch with the vitality that still courses so strongly through the piece, is, in this case, *le droict chemin,* the right road to authenticity. There are many choices to be made and there will be many people with little or no idea of them who will be only too ready to adopt stances. These you don't have to believe.

Monteverdi: *L'incoronazione di Poppea*

Since they began to reach a wider public in the 1960s, there has been a great deal of controversy over the way the operas of Monteverdi and his younger contemporaries, such as Cavalli and Cesti, should be brought back to life in our time. Many talk and write about the subject, but very few of those – and still fewer of the people who come to listen – know what the problems are, what part the revivifier actually plays and to what degree he has to enter into the original creative process to reveal the authentic voice.

From the beginning of the seventeenth century until the 1680s, when success and commercialism radically changed its format, opera was always written down in the same way. There was never anything approaching a full score as we know it today. The libretto was set to music mostly on two staves showing the voice part and the bass line. The latter is rarely rhythmic and mainly intended to indicate the harmonies. Occasionally there is a *ritornello* (an instrumental section, usually for strings) in three or five parts, sometimes begun but not finished, sometimes indicated perhaps by a *segue ritornello* but with no music. Even more occasionally some indication is given of instruments playing with the voices. That is all. Figs. 1 to 3 – from Monteverdi, Cesti and Cavalli – are typical.

The reasons for so skeletal an initial concept were simple and extremely practical. It was an intelligently conceived, almost ideal way of putting drama and music together in a rehearsable way which left options open for ideas to occur during the long period of preparation before the opera finally reached the stage. The method worked especially well in the earlier years of opera when the composer was always present at rehearsals. The two-line format made any reshaping, cutting, transposition or adaptation extremely easy. Imagine trying to take a few bars out of *Tristan*. It would unravel like a piece of knitting sheared off by scissors, so complex is the score on its 40 staves.

Like all the great seventeenth-century painters, the composers of early opera had their pupils and assistants around them to carry out their masters' instructions, fill in a few spaces, add a bar here or there, do transpositions, score others or complete a ritornello, and act as general factotums in the weeks that were always allocated for such preparation. It is touching to think of Cavalli helping Monteverdi in the initial creation of *Poppea*. In the single manuscript left in Venice (there is another, later one in Naples, and that is all) the celebrated last duet is almost certainly in Cavalli's hand and it may be that he

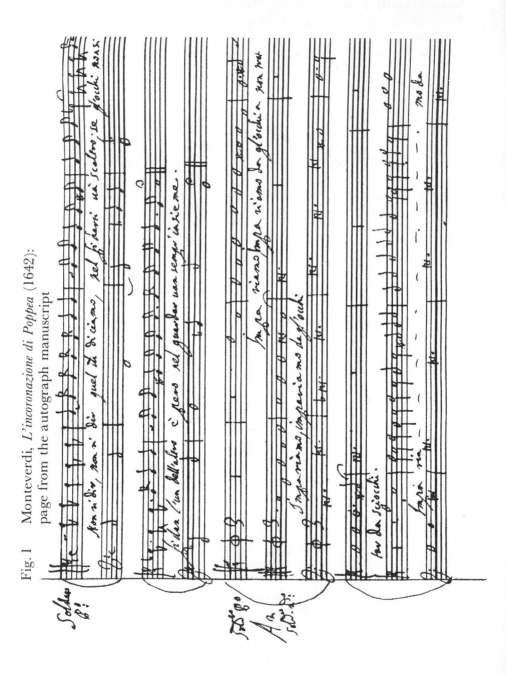

Fig. 1   Monteverdi, *L'incoronazione di Poppea* (1642): page from the autograph manuscript

Fig. 2   Cesti, *L'Argia* (1655): page from the autograph manuscript

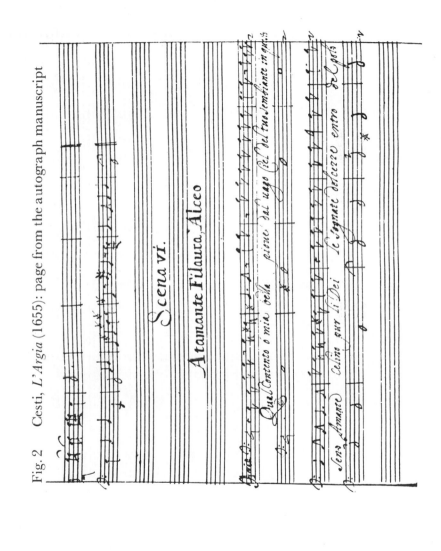

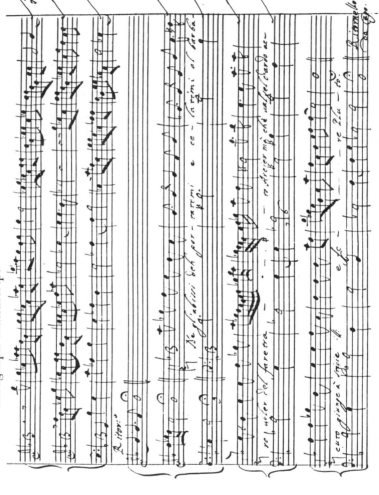

Fig. 3 Cavalli, *Scipione affricano* (1664): page from the autograph manuscript

even composed it himself. He certainly copied the idea later and wrote several final duets of great beauty in his own operas.

Conjecture as we may, there is clear evidence of collaboration and cooperation in many of these early operas, just as in many paintings of the time. The idea offends or alarms those who romantically view the creation of such works as an almost sacred revelation springing complete from a single author's mind, like soldiers from dragons' teeth. Academics become very nervous with the idea of collaboration, for apart from the uncertainty, the ascribing and cataloguing become very problematic and the footnotes plentiful.

But if we are to accept the responsibility of making these skeletal scores come alive we must approach the two lines left to us with an awareness of the theatre that is in them, as well as the fantastically vivid musical response that opera drew from Monteverdi. We must serve as his pupils and assistants did, and casting care aside – though not respect – use every sort of knowledge that scholarship can provide and participate in the creativity we sense contained within the score. It is like a love affair. You either give yourself to it wholeheartedly or you should give it up.

In the case of *Poppea* the problems of text are minor. There is the printed libretto of Busenello and the two manuscripts, of which the earlier one in Venice must take precedence. We know the constitution of the orchestra in principle from account books and contemporary observation. Essentially it was divided into two groups which, though able to play at the same time when necessary, fulfilled separate functions. There was a small group of strings which, due to the exigencies of ensemble, usually played when the music was metrical and only very occasionally in rhythmically freer moments of heightened recitative (as at the end of the prison scene in Cavalli's *L'Ormindo*). Fulfilling the major role of accompanying the passionate, expressive recitative which carries most of the drama, and was the most striking innovation of *Le nuove musiche* (as the new operatic style was called), is the continuo.

By continuo is meant something that literally provides a continuum under a solo line, a connecting link above which the voices may unfold the drama, revealing their emotions and characters. It comprised in Monteverdi's time a large group of instruments all separately suited to the accompaniment of freely expressive singing, unconstrained by the rigours of regular metre. We know that the group consisted of one or more of the following: reed and flue portative organs, lutes, guitars, theorbos, chitarrones, harpsichords

43

and harps, sometimes supported by sustaining 'cello lines played by single instruments.

So we may establish the principles of the way the voices were accompanied. For the bulk of the opera the continuo group did it, with the strings added at emotionally heightened moments, when metrical music, incipient arias, tended to appear. (The aria eventually grew in importance while the recitative became increasingly perfunctory and inexpressive.) The strings also played sinfonias and ritornellos where needed. The notes they would be required to play do not always appear in the manuscript.

There is a further principle for the use of the continuo to be deduced. Each of the instruments of which the group is comprised has a special tone-colour of its own. The variety of sound in the harpsichord and the harp are well known; the open pipes of the flue organ make a dulcet sound quite different from the darker, harsher sounds of the reed organ. The lute family varies from the bright, plangent sounds of the smaller instruments to the warm, round sounds of the guitar and the deep sonorities of the chitarrone. In *Orfeo* (1607) Monteverdi indicated in the score (printed not so much for performance as for presentation) how by selecting different instruments for different personages they could be used to enhance characterization. *Caronte canta al suono del regale* – Charon sings to the sound of a reed organ; the Messenger to a flue organ with chitarrone; for Orpheus' echo song two flue organs and two chitarrone placed at opposite sides of the stage. So successful is this use of instrumental colour for characterization in this, Monterverdi's first opera, that there could be no question but that in it he established a principle that continued for as long as recitative played as important a part in the form.

The strings, whenever scored in full, are in three or five parts, and herein lies another source of controversy. There is an enormous difference between the thin three-part texture and the rich, sensuous five-part sound. We are now used to a four-part texture and it is hard to imagine the difference in quality which even the addition of one single line, an inner second viola part, makes. Composers of consort music, madrigals and church music thought most often in five parts. Apart from its richness of sonority, this probably had something to do with complete final chords at cadences. (Following sixteenth-century contrapuntal practice the leading note could not descend to the fifth of the next chord; this only became acceptable in the four-part writing of Bach's and Handel's time. In five parts these cadential chords can more easily be made complete within the older discipline.)

44

Therefore, although a three-part texture may possibly have been used from time to time, I believe the most usual one was in five parts. Lully, who learned his operatic trade in seventeenth-century Italy, demonstrated all his life what was probably general practice there in his youth. In virtually all the instrumental music of his operas he wrote down three parts only, leaving two middle staves to be completed (often horribly) by his pupils and assistants. Examples to be found in the scores of Cavalli and Cesti only serve to confirm this view.

We should next examine what sort of precedent and licence there is in the matter of transposition and cutting. The manuscript of *Poppea*, like almost all the surviving working scores of early seventeenth-century Italian opera, has a number of cuts indicated, and a multitude of directions for transpositions *all' 4a, all' 5a, come sta, un tuon più alta*, all bespeaking, as one might expect from this method of producing opera, considerable latitude in the treatment of the material first put down on paper.

The last major problem to consider before beginning to bring the work back to musical and theatrical life is that of the bass line. In the manuscript it is rarely figured to indicate the harmony and, unless the vocal line shows some rhythmic cohesion or pattern, it is written almost entirely in white notes that fill the bar. These do not mean necessarily that the notes are to be sustained for their full length, but that a note so indicated is the basis for the harmony for as long as it lasts in the manuscript. Where and when it stops or acquires further pattern to emphasize meaning would have been up to the continuo player, and is now up to the person who 'realizes' the work for public performance. The actual harmonies used can only be determined by someone who knows, from the madrigals, church music, ballets and every scrap of more fully-scored music for instruments or voices, what is likely. There is no short cut for the application of this sort of skill or knowledge.

So we return to the manuscript, over 300 years after it was written, and begin our quest for its content. As an example of one approach I will take a single scene, the quarrel between Seneca and Nero, and describe in some detail the thoughts and decisions that went into one way of making it a viable piece of theatre for twentieth-century listeners.

In the opera, Poppea's growing domination over Nero is already established, as is Seneca's sympathy with the neglected empress, Ottavia. Nero encounters the ageing philosopher, once his mentor, and, like a truculent pupil, blurts out his intention of banishing his empress and marrying Poppea. Seneca answers respectfully, somewhat at length, but calmly attempting to make his impetuous emperor see reason. To every point Seneca makes Nero gives increasingly heated answers, betraying a wilful immaturity that eventually results in the unworthy accusation that Ottavia is frigid and barren. At this point Seneca himself begins to lose his temper and the interchanges become shorter and more violent until Nero – beaten in all but imperatorial authority – storms out, saying 'get out of my sight, you impertinent philosopher, insolent pedagogue.' It is a measure of the innate theatrical quality of the libretto and its setting that, in spite of his command, it is Nero who leaves, while Seneca stays to reflect calmly to the audience how power corrupts reason.

Fig. 4 shows how Monteverdi first wrote down the scene in his score.

The manuscript paper Monteverdi used had only ten staves and was expensive. To economize on space, as each character ends a speech the last bar is completed with a final bass-note and a concluding bar-line. The next character is then announced and new clefs are drawn before his phrase is set to music. The process is then repeated. However, in performance to stop and start with each new speech would stultify the dramatic flow and, from the way each voice enters in the key of the previous singer, it is clear that they were intended to follow each other naturally without breaks, depending on the meaning and intention of the words. The phrases are there to be fitted like a jigsaw puzzle into the dramatic scheme of things, emphasizing the *crescendo* of tension that finally erupts into anger on Seneca's part and hysteria on Nero's.

As it stands the scene is a long one, too long if we are to make the entire opera work within the normal span of present-day opera-going. Moreover, it is repetitive once the pattern of exchange between emperor-pupil and philosopher-mentor is established. Once Nero has told Seneca (and us) what he has come for and Seneca urges on him the folly of his wishes and respect for Roman law, there is no need to discuss that law. (Busenello was a lawyer and doubtless found it wonderfully fascinating.) It makes more dramatic sense for Nero immediately to change ground and say:

'We won't discuss it. I will have my way.'

Then Seneca can produce other reasons:

'Do not irritate the people or the Senate.'

Nero doesn't care about the people or the Senate;

Seneca: 'Then care about yourself and your reputation.'

Nero: 'If anyone dares to say anything I'll tear his tongue out.'

Seneca: 'The more silent you make them, the more they'll talk.'

Nero: 'Ottavia is frigid and barren.'

Seneca: 'Those in the wrong always seek other excuses.'

Nero: 'Force is law in time of peace . . .'

    Seneca: 'Force feeds hatred . . .'

(Nero) 'as the sword is in war . . .'

    (Seneca) 'and leads to bloodshed . . .'

(Nero) 'and has no need of reason.'

    (Seneca) 'Reason rules both men and the Gods.'

(Pause)

Nero: 'You! You risk my displeasure. In spite of you, in spite of the senate, Ottavia, Heaven and Hell, just or unjust, I will have my way today and Poppea shall be my wife.'

Seneca: 'That a woman should have the power to lead you to such error is a fault worthy neither of an emperor nor a demi-God; it is plebeian.'

Nero: 'Get out of my sight, you impertinent philosopher, insolent pedagogue.' *(exits)*

Seneca: 'Matters will always, always worsen when force contests the claims of reason.'

The early part of the encounter must clearly be free, and probably conceived in performance as being in two tempi: Nero rapid, eager and nervous; Seneca, calm by nature and intention, at a slower pace. It seemed to me suitable for Nero to be accompanied by harpsichord and 'cello playing *staccato* chords, Seneca by harp, reed organ and bass playing softly and sustained until he begins to lose his temper. When the music moves into connected, regular metre as tempers rise ('Force is law in time of peace'), the strings can enter and, reflecting the character of the continuo instruments, I used the upper strings for Nero and the lower for Seneca. The rhythms connect and join with a musical logic that brings us up to Nero's major explosion. Seneca regains his self-control, and the quiet of the reed organ and bass emphasize the deadly effectiveness of his final rebuke, which causes the hysterical rage of Nero's last lines. Seneca's final moving, sorrowful observation is metrical, so I again used the lower strings with the reed organ to express the growing calm of the old man as he realizes he will die for his opposition to Nero and for his faith in reason.

Fig. 5 shows the complete realization.

Fig. 4   Monteverdi, *L'incoronazione di Poppea*: Act 1, scene 9,
autograph manuscript

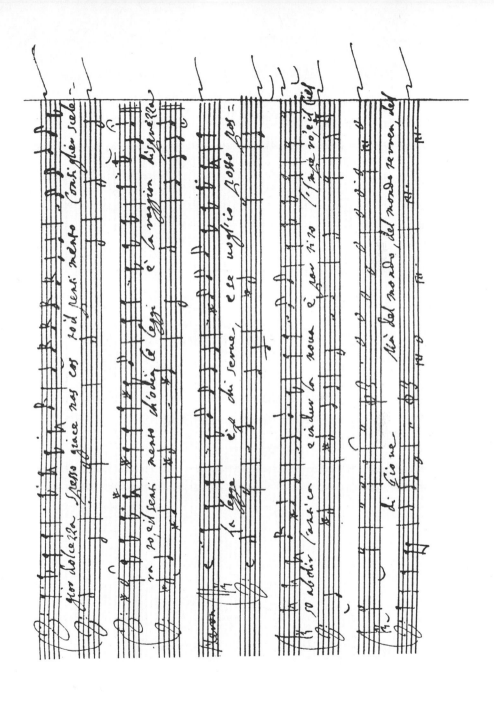

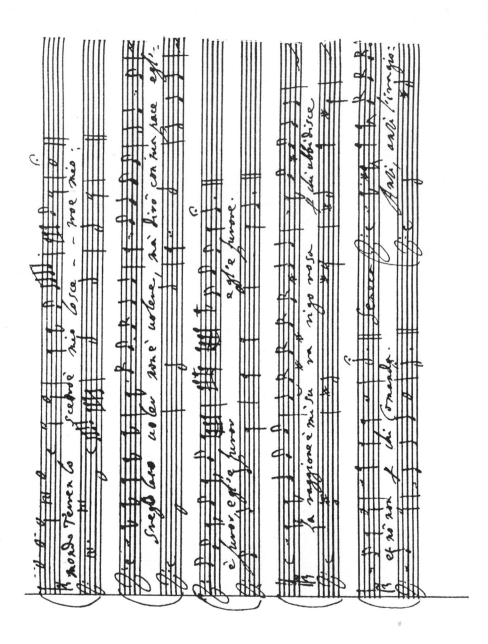

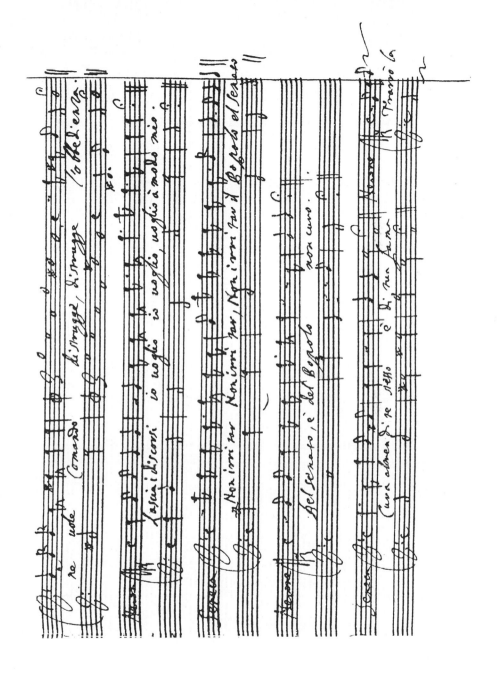

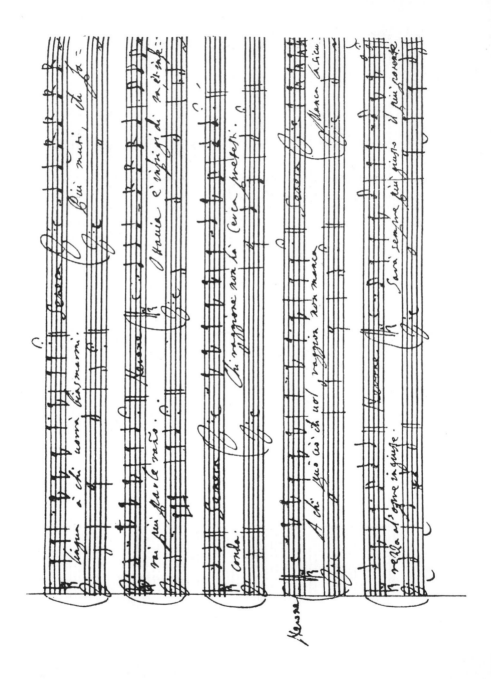

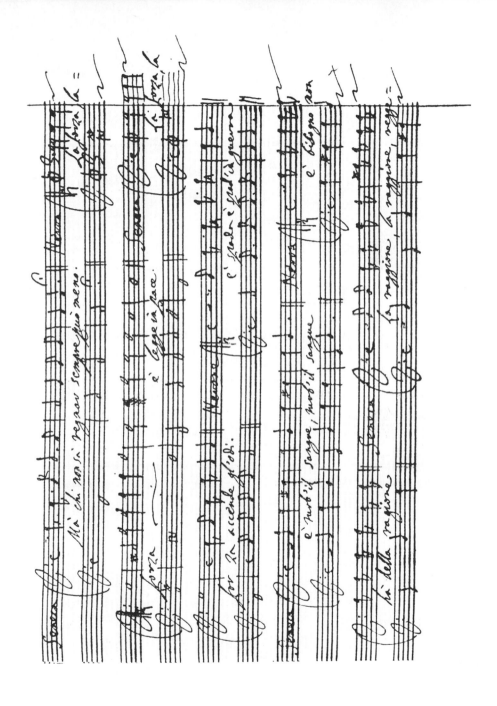

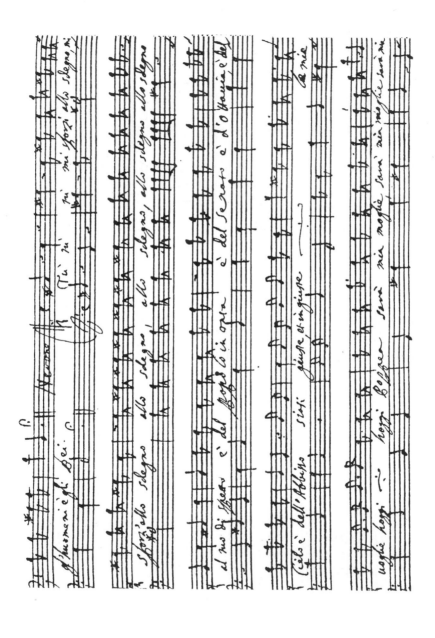

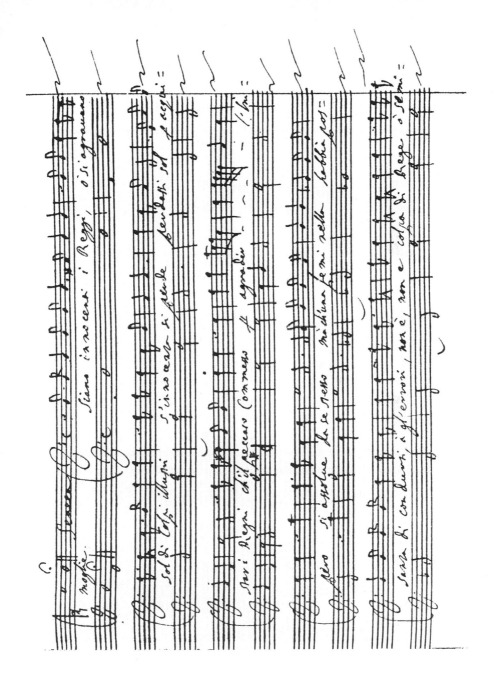

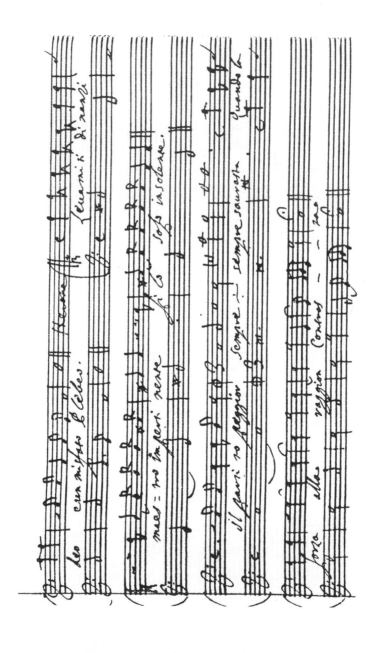

Fig. 5   Monteverdi, *L'incoronazione di Poppea*: Act 1, scene 9, author's realization

NERONE

-pe - - a.
-pe - - a.

SENECA

Si - gnor, nel fon - do al - la mag-
My lord, be-neath— what seems the

Harp
Reed Organ

_p_

Second Double Bass Continuo
(Second Cello Continuo tacet)

SENECA

-gior dol - cez - za spes - so gia - ce na - sco - sto il penti-men - to.
great - est plea - sure, there will of - ten lie hid - den bleat repen - tance

SENECA

Con - si - glier sce - la - ra - to è'l sen - ti - men - to, cho' dia le
Our e - mo - tions are pro - fli - gate ad - vi - sers that hate law and

NERONE

La-scia i di-scorsi,
No time for lectures

SENECA

leg - gi, e la ra - gion di - sprez - za.
jus - tice and will des - pise all rea - son.

First Harpsichord

f

First Cello Continuo

First Bass Continuo

Io vo-glio, io vo-glio vo-glio amo - do mi - o.
I will, yes I will, yes I will have it my way.

Non ir - ri-tar, non ir-ri-
Do not en-rage, do not en-

Harp
Reed Organ *f*

Second Double Bass Continuo
(Second Cello Continuo tacet)

NERONE

Del Se-na-to e del
For the Senate and the

SENECA

-tar, non ir-ri-tar il po—po-lo e'l Se-na-to.
-rage, do not en-rage the Sen—ate and the People.

First Harpsichord

f

First Cello Continuo

First Double Bass Continuo

po-po-lo   non cu—ro.
Peo-ple   I care not.

Cura al-me-no te stes-so,   e
Care, at least for yourself, sir,   and

Harp

Reed Organ   *mf*

Second Double Bass Continuo
(Second Cello Continuo tacet)

NERONE

Trar-rò la lin - gua   a chi vor - rà   bia-
Who-e-ver blames me,   I'll have them tear   his

SENECA

la   tua   fa - ma.
for   your   ho - nour.

First Harpsichord

(loco)

col 8va - - - - - - - - - -
First Cello Continuo
First Double Bass Continuo

-smarmi.   ot -
tongue out!   p   ot -

Più mu - ti che fa - rai,   più par-le - ran-no.
The more   of them you si - lence the more shall curse you.

First Harpsichord
p

(Harp tacet)
Reed Organ

Second Double Bass Continuo
(Second Cello Continuo tacet)

NERONE

8 -ta - via è in frigi-di ———— ta è tin-te-con-da.
-ta - via is both bar - ren— and fri-gid.

SENECA

Chi ra-gio-ne non
All who wish to do

Reed Organ,
Harp

Second Double Bass
Continuo
(Second Cello Continuo
tacet)

pp

First Cello Continuo
First Double Bass Continuo

64 (♩=104)

La for-za, la for - za, la for-za la for-
My po-wer, my po - wer, my po-wer, my po -

ha, cer - ca pre - te - sti
wrong search for a pre - text.

Orchestra strings
f Second Harpsichord

(Harp, Reed Organ,
Second Double Bass Continuo tacet)

NERONE

e bi-so-gno non ha del-la ra-gio-ne.
and they nei-ther have a-ny need of rea-son.

SENECA

tur-bail san-gue,
la ra-gio-ne, la ra-
It is reason, on-ly

65 (♩=92)

Tu,   tu,
You,   you,

-gio-ne reg-ge gl'huo-mi-nie gli De-i.
rea-son rules the earth and gods in hea-ven.

Orchestra strings

Second
Harpsichord

p

p

(Double Bass tacet)

NERONE

tu mi sfor-zial-lo sde-gno, mi sforziallo sdegno, al-lo sdegno al-lo
you, you brave my displea-sure, you brave my displeasure, my displeasure, my dis-

fp   fp cresc.

f

(♩=108) e poco accel.

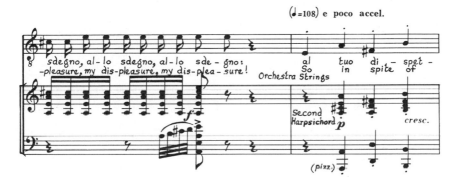

sdegno, al-lo sdegno, al-lo sde-gno: al tuo di-spet-
-pleasure, my dis-pleasure, my dis-plea-sure! So in spite of

Orchestra Strings

Second
Harpsichord p   cresc.

(pizz.)

-to, e del po-polo in on-ta, e del Se-na-to, e d'Ot-tavia, e del Cielo, e del l'A-
you, and in spite of the Senate and of the People, and Ot-tavia, and of Heaven and of

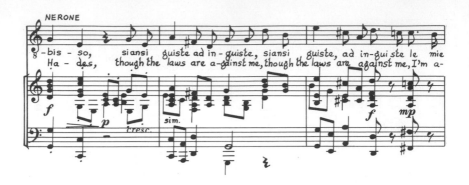

NERONE

-bis - so, siansi giuste ad in-giuste, siansi giuste, ad in-giuste le mie

Ha - des, though the laws are a-gainst me, though the laws are against me, I'm a-

voglie, hog - gi, hog - gi, hog-gi, Poppe-a sa-rà mia moglie, sarà mia

-bove them and I say tomor-row to-morrow Poppe - a shall be my wife, she

|66|

moglie, sarà mia mo - glie.

shall be my wife, she shall be.

SENECA

Ma ch'una femmi-nel-la habbia pos-

Oh, that a silly woman's po-wershould

Harp
Reed Organ

Second Double Bass Continuo
(Second Cello Continuo tacet)

Il parti-to peggior sem - pre, sem - pre, sem - pre so-
Now I fear for the worst al - ways, al - ways dark is the

Reed Organ

Orchestra Violas, Cellos,
Double Basses

-vra - sta, quan - do la for - za al - la - la
sea - son, when love of po - wer con - tests-

(Reed Organ tacet)

- ra - gion — con - tra - - - - - sta.
- the — claims — of — Rea - - - - - son.

Thus out of two staves of music is a scene recreated, delineating character, furthering the action and involving the listeners in the emotional tensions that grow through it as part of the broader structure of the opera. The notes, sounds and colours all have that in view, and I would urge singers and players always to communicate these tensions to the full so that, as Follino observed at the first performance of Monteverdi's *Arianna* in Mantua, the opera may be performed with so much emotion in so moving a way that no one hearing it is left unmoved.

Handel: *Acis and Galatea*
This is one of the best works Handel composed during his early years in England, and is also one that vexes those who favour the high and narrow road to authenticity, as well as those who risk the lower, broader way. The facts are relatively simple, and the difficulties depend on a basic initial choice.

Entitled variously 'Serenata', 'Pastoral Opera' and 'Masque', *Acis* was written in 1718 while Handel was house-composer to the Duke of Chandos at Cannons, a great mansion (alas, no longer standing) by James Gibbs near Edgware just north of London. It was composed for four soloists – soprano, two tenors and a bass – and chorus in the unusual five-part texture of soprano, three tenors and bass. This is the same combination of voices we find in the anthems Handel wrote for the ducal chapel, and we may assume that the choir doffed their cassocks for the occasion. Handel probably used a group of single instruments as accompaniment. Two oboes doubling recorders, probably a bassoon, two violins, 'cello, bass (or second 'cello) and harpsichord: eight or nine players in all.

For those following the high road this is the only way to perform the work, and some critics with but a peripheral knowledge of the facts are only too eager to leap into censorious print when it is otherwise presented. Which is a pity, for Handel himself did so on many occasions and on a much larger scale than at Cannons. These performances came about because the work was becoming popular in other people's hands, notably those of Thomas Arne senior, and Handel had no intention of losing such profits as were to be gained from his own composition.

On the lower road difficulties arise because the composer left very little evidence to show how he transformed the original score into one performable by 'a great number'. The first of his own performances after Cannons, at the King's Theatre in 1732, was announced as being 'now revived by him [Handel] with several additions and to be performed by a *great number of the best voices and instruments*'. It was an enormous success, and Handel went on performing it in various large-scale versions for ten years.

At Cannons he had had no option but to write for very small forces, and it is arguable that he himself felt that, performed in that way, the music was inadequately supported, at least in its more robust movements. Moreover, it would nowadays seem regrettably exclusive and certainly questionable to decry in the name of 'authenticity' modern performances on a grander scale, depriving larger choruses and orchestras, as well as audiences, the experience of so stunningly beautiful a work.

The history of the different versions that Handel made involving transposition, alterations, cuts, additions and even changes of cast, is daunting in its complexity. Nor is so elaborate a survey worthwhile, for in the end, as with *Messiah*, you only come up with a list of what happened when, with little or no deduced authority for what should happen now. The options are, of course, important; the facts of them are not. We have to survey the possibilities, possess some familiarity with Handel's music and some historical imagination, and make a passionate but modest commitment to the score we eventually come to perform. No small thing to ask. Much more, indeed, than the easier option of the narrow way, accepting the limitations of Cannons and performing the work on a small scale in a small place, something Handel himself never did again.

He left no full score of his later versions, and when *Acis* was printed by Walsh in 1743 the small-scale Cannons score was, basically, the one that the publisher reproduced with almost none of the additions the composer must subsequently have made. It nevertheless probably represents the movements and sequence of movements that Handel preferred.

Preparing a modern performance for larger forces means that we have to face the compromises that Handel himself faced in 1732. Viewed in this way it becomes an exciting challenge. Some of the numbers are so brilliantly scored for the original small combination that they are best left in that form, their special qualities being even enhanced by the larger sounds that surround them. Among these I would include Galatea's 'Hush, ye pretty warbling choir' and 'As when the dove laments his love'. Some numbers might benefit from being accompanied by a medium-sized group, less than the full band but larger than that at Cannons. Even with these one might adopt the practice of contrasting *concertino* and *ripieno*, as Handel often did. All three of Damon's arias would work well in this way, as would Acis's 'Where shall I seek the charming fair?', Galatea's 'Heart, the beat of soft delight' and Polyphemus's 'Ruddier than the cherry' – although this last might sound best (depending on circumstance) with solo instruments, so as to emphasize the humour of Handel's setting. Some numbers benefit greatly from larger-scale accompaniment: Acis's arias 'Love in her eyes sits playing' and 'Love sounds the alarm', Polyphemus's 'Cease to beauty', the duet 'Happy we' and the trio 'The flocks shall leave the mountains'.

The principle, at least, is clear. Each aria has to be presented in the way that will best reveal its character within the larger context, and the three-tier use of the orchestra will help both this and the dynamic contrasts of the drama they unfold.

All the choruses benefit from larger numbers of both voices and instruments, except perhaps the beginning of Act II, 'Wretched lovers', which might be more effective with solo voices until the entrance of Polyphemus.

Apart from the allocation of continuo instruments – bassoon, 'cello, bass, harpsichord and organ, judged in the context of the whole – there is the major problem of the violas, an essential part of the larger accompaniment for which there exists virtually no music. We have to do what Handel – or J.C. Smith, or a pupil – did: decide where they are needed and write a part for them. Handel would certainly not have hired players to perform for three minutes in 'Happy we' (whose scoring contains the only extant viola part) and sit around twiddling their thumbs for the rest of the evening. In most of the arias they are superfluous, but in all the accompanied recitatives they can add valuable harmonic support. The following example shows how their part might be in Galatea's recitative 'Ye verdant plains':

Recitativo

In choruses the viola line can support the tenors to great advantage, as well as fill out the tuttis. They certainly would have played in the brilliant opening Sinfonia (which also benefits from alternating *concertino* and *ripieno*). In such movements Handel generally had them playing an octave above the bass line, occasionally departing from it to provide harmonic support or to avoid rising above the violins. A typical version of the first bars might be as follows:

Sinfonia: **Presto**

Thus may we approach the preparation of *Acis and Galatea* for present-day performance in the form the composer himself most often gave it – and in doing so, hope to realize something of the authentic spirit held within this beautiful work.

There is no one way, no one solution to any of its problems, nor ever was there one. But the indecision stops when you come to performance: then there is only the way you have committed yourself to follow. The difference between the two views of authenticity becomes most clearly apparent in the preparation for that commitment. The one narrows down the possibilities, the other broadens them so that informed choice and compromise can play their part in liberating the vitality of the music.

CHAPTER SEVEN

THE HIGH ROAD, THE LOW ROAD

What, then, is this authenticity that has become so much the concern of all performers of music before 1800 and, equally, the focus of attention for critics and listeners?

It can only mean one thing: the clearest possible revelation of that music so that its intrinsic qualities, vitality and value are presented again as vividly as they may conceivably ever have been. So will the evidence of its power to transcend the years be strengthened, and the delight and elation that communication with things of the spirit brings be confirmed. In these lie the gifts of confidence and joy that encourage us to move more freely about the very dangerous terrain we currently inhabit.

In dispute, or at least confusion, are how and in what ways the revelation may best be achieved. There are those who believe that only as we come closer to the exact conditions, the precisely duplicated ways and means of music's first appearance, can its authentic message and content be revealed.

Then there are those who believe that the closer we come to knowing how and why it was written, why as well as how it was performed, the closer we shall come to the inner vitality of the composer's mind, the revelation of which to present-day audiences is more important than any other aspect of performance.

The two views have much in common, but in the last analysis they diverge greatly, finding themselves often on opposite sides of sometimes vituperative controversy. For the one, scholarship and historical research are the final arbiters; for the other, present communication of perceived vitality is the deciding factor. The one must, perforce, be exclusive and restrictive, as all true academic disciplines are. The other seeks the widest creative freedom within the disciplines that acquired knowledge imposes. The difference of intent is profound.

Authenticity in the first view eventually comes to resemble the mythological bird that flies around in ever-decreasing circles, eventually disappearing into its own feathers. Pursued logically, this concept of authenticity arrives at the dubious but inevitable conclusion that there is only one way perfectly to reveal a piece of earlier music. Yet in the stampede that has accompanied the widespread enthusiasm for things 'original' there has, so far, appeared no point at which that sort of authentic practice will deny itself the final absurdity. Sometimes it would seem that the closer people come to it, the louder they are applauded for doing so. Witness Stephen Plaistow in the *Gramophone* of May 1986 on a recent recording of the Mozart Clarinet Concerto: 'As R.F. [Roger Fiske] was saying in March, the time must be near when only basset (horn) versions of the Mozart Clarinet Concerto are acceptable at public concerts. For record collectors I think that moment has arrived.' How an intelligent person could come to write as absurdly bigoted an opinion as that is hard to imagine, but the example is by no means unique.

If Bach's cantata *Wachet auf* can finally only fully reveal its vitality by being played in St Thomas's Church, Leipzig, with the instruments and voices that the composer had at his disposal, and on the 27th Sunday after Trinity (which occurs very seldom, only twice in Bach's lifetime), we should hear it at its best very rarely indeed. The thesis is not as far-fetched as all that, for are there not frequent performances of *Messiah* that claim to reproduce exactly the numbers and conditions of its first appearance in Dublin – and to be superior on that account? Deceive ourselves as we may, the thesis of this first view without qualifications is as absurd as the proposition that a visit to Williamsburg, Virginia – where every house, every buggy, every costume, every aspect of its former life is reproduced quite perfectly – will show in any real sense what early American colonial life was like.

The most important reason why such propositions will eventually prove groundless is always the same. It is we who are different. Not only are time and, for all practical purposes, place dislocated in such narrow-visioned attempts at authenticity, but the very sensibilities by which we have to recognize validity are out of kilter with what people seek to represent in this way. Current speed, noise, media, the stimuli of the world around us, our own backgrounds, to say nothing of our acquired historical awareness have little in common with the original circumstances. None of these factors was present when 'early music' was first performed, and the eager search for 'authentic purity' along those lines begins to resemble the hoped-for fulfilment of that pathetic nun in Ronald Firbank's *Valmouth,* waiting for her dancing-day that came but once a year and, even so, did not achieve much among the penitential holly-bags, for no one really noticed her.

The nun may have had the gifts of a Fonteyn and danced perfectly: the music may be performed exactly where and as it had been conceived; but only one half, the historical half of the proposition will have been fulfilled. The ignoring of the differences between those who once listened and those who now listen means that the performer has abnegated or at least relegated to secondary importance his first responsibility as a communicator to the present.

Authenticity in the second view must embrace something the other abhors: compromise. This function of the mind, inescapable in almost every aspect of living, symbolizes for some vacillation and weakness of purpose. The nineteenth century, in its preoccupation with man's upward progress, saw compromise as a blemish upon possible perfection and became ashamed of it. It was put aside as if, like original sin, it were best ignored; pretending, if it showed, that it didn't exist. All cults, religious and political as well as musical, tend to reject compromise as an unacceptable failing that mars the ideal, diminishes the particularity and weakens the message. It is the root cause of the fundamental unworkability of socialism, many of whose ideals are quite unexceptionable. Churchill is said once to have advised a fellow politician never to abandon his ideals but, equally, never to try to put them into practice.

Of course, it would have been the most amazing revelation to have heard *Wachet auf* in Leipzig under Bach's direction on 25 November 1731, but no amount of wishing will make it happen. We can only attempt to understand, from the text that is left to us and the knowledge of it that we can assemble, what it is that he was attempting to do and, subsequently, make as our prime objective a translation of that into our own time; not, primarily, a reproduction of what actually happened. So viewed, the compromise involved would seem neither impossible nor unprofitable, nor yet unworthy.

Compromise is not as discouraged as it once was. The acceptance that it is an unavoidable part of life has led many to understand that it can also be a productive, stimulating activity worth studying and mastering. In the confrontation between an ideal and its practice there is something illuminating to be found in the realization that it cannot be made fully to work. If, then, we embrace the idea of compromise, for it to be successful there must be nothing of inhibiting regret or guilt, or a sense of second-best or shame that we cannot achieve the 'purity' of the first intent, if indeed it was 'pure'. And, since it plays so precise a part in this second view of authenticity, it would be well to examine in what ways compromise may affect the revelation of music's value that we seek to transmit.

The fact that we live at a different pace from anything previously known, and are impatient of what we consider the tedium of excessive length, must be one cause for compromise. Occasionally we like extremes and can be persuaded to hear, for example, a Handel opera more complete than Handel probably ever heard it himself. Ordinarily, however, opera-houses cannot mount works that last five hours, nor would the general public be persuaded in the ordinary way to listen for so long. To deprive them of Handel's operas on that account seems a high price to pay when there is a perfectly viable alternative.

The way compromise may be effected can change. There was a time when all manner of snippings were made to keep Handel's operas within bounds. Now that the *da capo* aria is recognized as an inviolable eighteenth-century form, snippings are out and it is whole arias, or even scenes, that have to go. Both methods proved effective for their time, and we should be cautious about stating that one is absolutely better than the other. It may be that our latest solutions, too, will change as a result of the needs and wishes of another time.

Tempi present another variable element in the process of older music's revitalization, one calling for compromises from which purer minds may shrink. But truly there can be no absolute speeds, only ideas of speed which will vary according to numbers, place, acoustics and occasion. This must always have been the case, despite diligent research and strong opinion to the contrary.

A further reason for compromise is that all music before 1800 was created for a restricted public which did not travel much, had national characteristics, local expectations and customs all of which surrounded and influenced it. When the music is played or sung on a world-wide scale today, these elements have to be understood, dealt with and in some way incorporated or deliberately ignored.

But the most important function of compromise as it affects us today lies in the absorption of what the newest manifestation of our quest for the truth has to show us. I speak of 'original' instruments.

There can be no question of abandoning the instruments in general use (which will in their turn develop new characteristics and change). It would be pie in the sky to think otherwise, for music would become divided into historical segments, each with its own brand of performer. There is, nevertheless, a world of influence to be absorbed, digested and resolved into modern practice through the work of those who have devoted themselves to the exploration of the particular techniques involved in playing these instruments.

Apart from differently focused sounds, the effects of lower pitch, narrower dynamic range, possibilities of bowing, the quality of vibrato and the generally frailer tone quality, by far the most important revelation, and the one that has and will have the greatest impact on performance, is that of articulation: the infinite variety in degree of separation; the importance of the dynamic structure of the phrases so exposed; and the discovery that, far from splitting the music into pieces, this newly-revealed old element of performance may serve to expound the larger framework in earlier music in a way that the long lines appropriate to Wagner and Brahms cannot do.

It becomes totally absorbing to see what light this can shed on the performance of, say, the Haydn symphonies or the early music of Beethoven, whose players for the *Eroica* symphony (1803) regularly performed for Haydn and Mozart, and in a style that Beethoven might disrupt but would not have questioned. To conceive his music as if he had already invented Brahms, if not Mahler, is the way whole generations have previously played and thought of it, providing the musical counterpart to the awe-inspiring image the late nineteenth century created for him. Right for them, no doubt, but wrong for us, if still not all of us.

So do our views change, and I would again raise the question as to whether we should consider them better on that account; or if that is not yet another vestige of nineteenth-century philosophy that hangs about our minds.

We rarely hear Casals' playing of the Bach suites or Wanda Landowska's playing of the '48' extolled today. Yet in their time those artists communicated the vitality of that music wonderfully, and we are not so far removed in time that, with a little exercise of musical empathy, we cannot understand why it was so. We would not play in their way today; but it is not that the style of playing was wrong, merely that the circumstances surrounding it have changed, with new influences, new pressures and new thoughts requiring different sets of compromises in bringing the music to life.

For whatever reason, we feel a strong need to get as close as possible to the original sources of music, to separate them out into periods and styles and to be able to sense the difference in our performance of them. Here lies the most significant division between the two views of how it should be done. The one seeks to pin the various periods of music to their sources where they may be exhibited for ever, like stuffed animals: for every problem there is one best solution. The other accepts, even enjoys the idea that time changes expectations and needs. The rewards of performance are to be found in constant revision and reinterpretation to keep pace with the present as much as to keep faith with the past. The rewards of the listener are in the new aspects of the music's vitality that these changes continually reveal.

This broader way is complex and difficult. It must embrace the results of research, the conditions of present-day performance and all the compromise that that entails, doing so without losing or betraying the content of the music as we perceive it. The problems will never cease, but they are such that their resolution can bring joy and fulfilment to performer and listener alike. When the inhibitions and restrictions of false authenticity are felt, or even the self-indulgence of undisciplined compromise, then the wrong road has been taken.

Seriousness of purpose combined with the acquisition of knowledge; a never-ending revision of the probabilities and possibilities; a passionate modesty; these are the requisites for allowing the creativity we sense in the music to flourish. In this way we shall, I believe, discover the true meaning and importance of authenticity for our time.

NOTES

Chapter 1

1 *Handel's Dramatic Oratorios and Masques* (1959), p.144
2 *The History of Music in England* (1907), p.197
3 *The Evolution of the Art of Music* (1896), p.165
4 Burney: *A General History of Music from the Earliest Ages to the Present Period*, Vol. IV (London, 1789), p.590
5 *Ibid.*, p.593
6 *Ibid.*, p.594
7 *Ibid.*, p.595
8 *Birmingham Gazette*, Sept. 1829
9 A.D.Coleridge, *Reminiscences*, ed. J.A.Fuller-Maitland (1921)

Chapter 2

1 The idea is not dead. A recent programme note (1986) on Beethoven's *Eroica* observed that 'In creating his Third Symphony, Beethoven eroded all the old spatial constraints of the genre, leaving the eighteenth century in the archives of history.'
2 *Progress, its Laws and Cause* (1857), Conclusion
3 *Social Statics* (1850), Part 1, Chapter 2
4 The very title of Wagner's book is derived from Feuerbach's *The Philosophy of the Future* (1843)
5 *Gesammelte Schriften* (1872), Vol. III, p.39
6 *A General History of Music* (1886), p.411
7 *Ibid.*, p.412
8 *Ibid.*, pp.471-2
9 *A History of Music in England* (1907), p.357
10 *The Evolution of the Art of Music* (1896), p.336
11 *Ibid.*, p.337

Chapter 3

1   *A General History of Music from the Earliest Ages to the Present Period,*
    Vol. IV (London, 1789), p.27
2   *The Evolution of the Art of Music* (1896), p.157
3   *Ibid.,* p.158
4   *Ibid.,* p.194
5   *Ibid.,* p.167
6   *Ibid.,* p.248
7   *Ibid.,* p.226
8   *Ibid.,* p.228
9   *Ibid.,* p.255
10 *Ibid.,* p.256
11 *Ibid.,* p.272
12 *Ibid.,* p.273
13 *Ibid.,* p.259
14 *Ibid.,* p.269
15 *Ibid.,* p.273
16 *Ibid.,* p.275
17 *Ibid.,* p.303
18 *Ibid.,* p.331
19 *Ibid.,* p.333
20 *Ibid.,* p.336
21 *Ibid.,* p.250

Chapter 5

1   *Musical Ornamentation,* Novello, Ewer & Co. Music Primer (1893-5)

Chapter 6

1   'Berlioz: the Best of Both Worlds', *Cambridge Opera Handbooks:*
    C.W. von Gluck, ed. Patricia Howard, p.101
2   *Ibid.,* p.102